RECREATION & TOURISM INITIATIVE

An Assessment of Frameworks Useful for Public Land Recreation Planning

Stephen F. McCool, Roger N. Clark,
and George H. Stankey

General Technical Report
PNW-GTR-705
March 2007

 United States
Department of
Agriculture

 Forest
Service

 Pacific Northwest
Research Station

The **Forest Service** of the U.S. Department of Agriculture is dedicated to the principle of multiple use management of the Nation's forest resources for sustained yields of wood, water, forage, wildlife, and recreation. Through forestry research, cooperation with the States and private forest owners, and management of the national forests and national grasslands, it strives—as directed by Congress—to provide increasingly greater service to a growing Nation.

The U.S. Department of Agriculture (USDA) prohibits discrimination in all its programs and activities on the basis of race, color, national origin, age, disability, and where applicable, sex, marital status, familial status, parental status, religion, sexual orientation, genetic information, political beliefs, reprisal, or because all or part of an individual's income is derived from any public assistance program. (Not all prohibited bases apply to all programs.) Persons with disabilities who require alternative means for communication of program information (Braille, large print, audiotape, etc.) should contact USDA's TARGET Center at (202) 720-2600 (voice and TDD).

To file a complaint of discrimination write USDA, Director, Office of Civil Rights, 1400 Independence Avenue, S.W. Washington, DC 20250-9410, or call (800) 795-3272 (voice) or (202) 720-6382 (TDD). USDA is an equal opportunity provider and employer.

Authors

Stephen F. McCool is a professor of Wildland Recreation Management, Department of Society and Conservation, University of Montana, Missoula, MT 59812; **Roger N. Clark** and **George H. Stankey** are research social scientists (retired), U.S. Department of Agriculture, Forest Service, Pacific Northwest Research Station. Clark was at the Pacific Wildland Fire Sciences Laboratory, 400 N 34th, Suite 201, Seattle, WA 98103, and Stankey was at the Forestry Sciences Laboratory, 3200 SW Jefferson Way, Corvallis, OR 97331.

Cover photo by Stephen F. McCool.

Abstract

McCool, Stephen F.; Clark, Roger N.; Stankey, George, H. 2007. An assessment of frameworks useful for public land recreation planning. Gen. Tech Rep. PNW-GTR-705. Portland, OR: U.S. Department of Agriculture, Forest Service, Pacific Northwest Research Station. 125 p.

Public land managers are confronted with an ever-growing and diversifying set of demands for providing recreation opportunities. Coupled with a variety of trends (devolution of governance and decisionmaking, population growth, technological innovation, shifts in public values, economic restructuring) and reduced organizational capacity, these demands represent a significant and complex challenge to public land management. One way of dealing with this situation is to use a framework to assist in working through this complexity. A framework, for the purpose of this report, is a process using a set of steps, based on sound science, that assists managers in framing a particular problem, working through it, and arriving at a set of defendable decisions. Several such frameworks exist for providing recreation opportunities on public lands. These include the Recreation Opportunity Spectrum, Limits of Acceptable Change, Visitor Experience and Resource Protection, Visitor Impact Management, and Benefits-Based Management. The report traces the development of each of these frameworks, describes the fundamental premises and concepts used within them, and provides an assessment of the experience with their use. Each of the frameworks has been used with varying success, depending on the organization's will, its technical capacity, the extent to which the process is inclusive of varying value systems, how open and deliberative the process is, the extent to which the organization is concerned with effectiveness, and the extent to which issues are confronted at the systems level.

Keywords: Recreation frameworks, planning, ROS, LAC, VERP, VIM, BBM.

Preface

This work represents an attempt to apply the experience and knowledge of the authors in addressing some of the complex and messy issues of public land recreation planning. We believe that understanding and successfully addressing these issues requires planners and managers to not only be aware of the large-scale trends and driving forces forming their decisionmaking environment, but also to understand the frameworks available to work through the issues confronting them. This paper contains not only a synthesis of appropriate literature, but also a reflection on our own experience in developing and implementing several of the frameworks discussed. In many of the sections of this paper, we provide insights and impressions that are not necessarily reported in the literature; for one thing, there is little literature that discusses the "how to's" of recreation planning, and for another, these statements are based on our personal experiences and evaluation of those experiences in many situations.

In reviewing literature, we emphasized manuscripts that can be retrieved relatively easily, and we did not attempt to include all literature on a particular topic. We have emphasized the earlier or more influential papers on planning frameworks. We believe that planning exists within a larger and turbulent environment; understanding that environment is helpful in understanding the relevancy and appropriateness of a particular framework and how it can be applied. This report does not have to be read from beginning to end, although that would be helpful; the assessment of each framework can be understood independently from the other parts of this work.

Contents

Chapter 1: Introduction

Federally administered public lands play increasingly important roles in providing settings for recreation experiences and tourism development. These lands have long supplied resource commodities, such as timber, grass, and minerals, for local industry. They continue to serve as the watersheds for community water supplies and function as habitat for a variety of plants and animals. However, growing interest in their role as a major foundation of tourism development, particularly for communities in transition from extraction-based economies, places new and more complex demands on public land managers.

As explained in chapter 2, a variety of social, economic, and political changes have led to an increasingly complex and contentious environment for responding to such demands. Not only are the economic stakes higher, but there is growing scrutiny and accountability in public land planning. These characteristics suggest that analysis of proposals, strategic policy, and project planning must rely more on frameworks and concepts that explicate decisions than in the past. Appropriate planning frameworks can help to avoid unnecessary impacts, duplication, and lost opportunities to ensure optimal benefits flow from public lands.

And although conceptual advances in land management, such as landscape ecology, coupled with technological improvements, such as geographic information systems, provide a greater capability for informing decisions, these changes have often led to greater visibility of the scientific uncertainty intrinsic to those decisions. The consideration of longer timeframes and larger spatial scales in decision analysis means that there is greater argument over what we think we know. Too, the recognition embedded within such fields as landscape ecology that systems tend to be nonlinearly dynamic brings complexity to the decisionmaking environment as well. These factors have converged to make it difficult for the public and agency staff to understand how decisions are made at a time when the public is demanding greater involvement in such decisions.

Recreation and tourism development are not immune from this situation. What once was perceived as a relatively "benign" use of public lands is now often as controversial as the timber sales it has replaced. Large-scale tourism developments, such as destination ski resorts, are frequently accompanied by a litany of problematic social effects in addition to the manifest environmental ones. Decisionmakers providing opportunities for recreation and tourism development are confronted with this increasing contentiousness, complexity, and uncertainty about the consequences of their decisions. Such decisionmakers are increasingly expected to scientifically justify plans and policies.

Appropriate planning frameworks can help to avoid unnecessary impacts, duplication, and lost opportunities to ensure optimal benefits flow from public lands.

The result of this socially and scientifically turbulent environment is a growing need for frameworks and concepts that assist decisionmakers in assembling a set of informed alternatives. Concepts that are useful to decisionmakers are ones that help clarify underlying conflicts, create understanding of the issues at stake, and build understanding of choices and consequences. Useful frameworks are those that help decisionmakers "work through" these choices in a manner that allows technical expertise, scientific knowledge, and public values and interests to be incorporated, assessed, and used. In this paper, we review the evolution of the principal frameworks available to assist decisionmakers in working through and understanding public land recreation opportunities. In addition, we provide a primer on their use.

Some Observations About Providing Recreation Opportunities on Public Lands

The provision of recreation on public lands within a dynamic, multidimensional, and uncertain context is complex, challenging, and fraught with potential misdirection and unanticipated consequences. For example, increased demand that public lands provide commercialized recreation opportunities have led to conceptualizing management as one of identifying a carrying capacity for recreation, and then allocating such capacity between commercial and public visitors. Such a simplistic representation of a complex problem (e.g., what opportunities to be provided, to whom, where, how, and with what consequences) follows from a lack of the organizational capacity needed to properly frame and respond to the problem. As in other areas of resource management, ideologies may subtly influence the approaches managers take to decisions about recreation on public lands.

We note that these decisions occur in a set of stages: policy, planning, and implementation (including monitoring). Logically, the former stages precede the latter, although in development and implementation in the seemingly chaotic world of natural resources, such a rational representation is probably inappropriate. We add here that the iterative nature of policy, planning, and implementation is quite appropriate in a world characterized by uncertainty, but it is the chaotic character of what actually occurs that makes decisions difficult to understand, follow and, in many cases, defend. At each of these stages, there may be frameworks and concepts that help managers clarify and understand the context and requirements for decisions. Appropriate frameworks help managers work through the decision process. By knowing what frameworks are available for what types of decisions and issues, managers can increase the quality of their decisions.

Public land recreation frameworks have been developed over the last 25 years. Such development was generally in response to specific planning and implementation issues, often derived out of formalized policy, such as the National Forest Management Act of 1976 (Forest Service), Federal Land Policy and Management Act of 1976 (UDSI Bureau of Land Management) or the General Authorities Act of 1978 (National Park Service). However, these frameworks were also often developed in response to problems and challenges that are somewhat different, and as Nilsen and Tayler (1997) argue, the first step in determining their suitability is to "decide which questions they are seeking to answer." For example, the Limits of Acceptable Change framework (Stankey et al. 1985) was developed in response to numerous failed attempts to establish recreational carrying capacities for components of the National Wilderness Preservation System.

There are a number of formal and informal processes that help managers make decisions, but which are not oriented toward recreation planning. These processes are for the most part, constructed around environmental assessment, such as environmental impact statement processes, social impact assessment, landscape and watershed assessment processes, integrated resource management, and so on. Although these processes are comprehensive in the sense of making alternative generation and assessment of consequences explicit, in themselves, they do not provide the substantive clarification and understanding of recreation and tourism that is needed in conducting these processes. Thus, our focus in this paper is on the specific frameworks and concepts developed to help clarify and create understanding about recreation and tourism on public lands. Our overall objective is to provide decisionmakers with an understanding of how such frameworks evolved, what issues they address, and the strengths and weaknesses of each. We initiate this presentation with a short discussion about the functions and rationale for recreation planning, as understanding why organizations plan is fundamental to assessing the frameworks available.

What Is Planning About?

There may be as many definitions of planning as there are planners, but probably the most widespread approach to a definition of planning is that it is a process to describe both a desired or acceptable future and the "best" route to it—leaving open the definition of best for the moment. Although other definitions range from "application of science to policy" (Faludi 1973) to "linking knowledge to action" (Friedmann 1973), the one we use here—see below—is probably the most widespread notion of the idea of planning.

Organizations plan for a number of reasons: to solve a problem, because they are told to do so, to reduce individual discretion, to maintain consistency, to control that which can be controlled, and so on. These notions may have been useful in the days of stability and predictability (if there ever were those days), but in an era, as typified in chapter 2, that is chaotic, dynamic, and filled with uncertainty, such concepts of planning do not seem to fit well. There are at least three weaknesses (Weick and Sutcliffe 2001) with those reasons for planning:

1. Plans are built from assumptions, and therefore contain expectations about the future; those expectations, however, filter out important, contradictory information such that data challenging the validity of those assumptions may never be observed.

2. Plans are contingencies based on what we expect to occur, and thus limit our repertoire of potential actions should our expectations not be met.

3. Planning processes presume that rational people, following the same process, will come to the same decisions; but in a world of complexity and uncertainty, such plans cannot accommodate the inevitable surprises and unexpected events that will occur.

The linear, unidirectional character of planning implied from formalized planning definitions and processes is not well-suited for the public land contexts within which recreation and tourism development occur.

The linear, unidirectional character of planning implied from formalized planning definitions and processes is not well-suited for the public land contexts within which recreation and tourism development occur. These settings are not only contentious, but are fluid as well: priorities shift, needs change, and problems and challenges evolve. In part, the notion of adaptive management (see Stankey et al. 2003a for a review) was developed to deal with the need for feedback and evaluation of decisions. Thus, a major dimension of suitable and appropriate recreation planning frameworks would be processes that provide feedback to managers. We view planning as an iterative, inclusive process where stakeholders and planners jointly frame issues, construct futures, and choose socially acceptable, efficient, equitable, and effective pathways to those futures. Thus, planning may be more formally defined as a process of identifying a desired future and determining the pathway (or set of pathways) to it.

The frameworks assessed in this paper do provide for such feedback, but, as noted earlier, the lack of feedback and evaluation is often a function of not only institutional design but also frequently of organizational will and priority. Feedback may well indicate that change in a management regime is needed, but hard won regimes are often difficult to change, even given good evidence for such a change.

What Functions Does a Planning Framework for Recreation and Tourism Serve?

Given the above, frameworks that focus on allocation decisions for recreation and tourism serve to provide some systematic process for making those decisions such that managers are fully aware of the desired future they wish to attain, the alternative routes to the future, the consequences of those alternatives, and the social acceptability of proposed management actions. In addition, these frameworks provide the explicitness and feedback needed in a time of change, complexity, and uncertainty. Stankey and Clark (1996) suggested that an effective framework would (1) identify tradeoffs between provision of recreation opportunities with the resulting local economic impacts and protection of biodiversity values, (2) appreciate and address complexity (rather than suggest reductionistic approaches), and (3) accommodate the array of constituencies with interests in the specific area or issue.

Finally, recreation and tourism planning frameworks make decisionmaking efficient by focusing attention on important elements of the political and social environment, effective by gaining the public support that is needed for implementation, and equitable by forcing consideration of who wins and who loses. In an overall sense, a framework increases the opportunities to practice the "mindfulness" Weick and Sutcliffe (2001) argued is important to deal with the inevitable surprises occurring in an uncertain context.

In this report, we examine and assess the principal concepts and frameworks that managers have available to assist in making decisions about recreation and tourism development opportunities. Many of these are a result of collaborative efforts between scientists and managers. Those efforts were largely in response to specific issues or policy initiatives for which a defensible, transparent, and logical approach was needed.

Organization of This Report

We begin the assessment by discussing in more detail the significant contextual changes and driving forces that have accelerated the need for recreation and tourism planning frameworks in recent years (chapter 2). Understanding this context is critical to application of the frameworks. We then turn to an overview of the frameworks that we have identified to briefly discuss their function and origin (chapter 3).

Following the overview, we provide a primer on the principal frameworks available to assist decisionmakers (chapter 4). The primer describes and evaluates the frameworks. The objective of the primer is to provide planners with enough information to decide which framework to use in a specific circumstance. The primer focuses on the Recreation Opportunity Spectrum and Limits of Acceptable Change as these are the best known and most widely applied frameworks, but others such as Visitor Impact Management, Visitor Experience and Resource Protection, and Benefits-Based Management are included, although not in the same depth. We have designed this report so that it is not necessarily meant to be read from beginning to end. Although chapter 2 provides a needed context for planning, one simply interested in the frameworks per se may only want to read chapter 4.

Chapter 2: The Context for Recreation Planning

The social, political, and legal environment within which planning and management take place today has changed markedly over the past several decades. Scarcely a generation ago, planning and management operated in a world in which it was presumed that problems were both well defined and agreed upon, those problems could be solved by technical-scientific investigation, and once defined and studied, the means to resolve them could be implemented in an efficient and cost-effective manner. Today, there is a growing realization that these conditions, if they ever did exist, are fast disappearing. The stable and predictable world of yesterday has been replaced by conditions of extraordinary turbulence—both sociopolitical and technical-scientific. Decisions must be made within a rapidly changing and pluralistic social context, and almost all these decisions are undertaken in the face of high levels of uncertainty regarding both causation and their relative effectiveness. In short, the world in which planners and managers operate today has changed in many fundamental ways.

These changes imply that approaches to planning and management once effective and appropriate are likely no longer so. Changes in the larger social, economic, and political context have led to new methods for planning and management; for example, the demand for inclusive public involvement processes, pressures for shared decisionmaking systems, and efforts to include a broader range of knowledge. Such changes are fundamental and systemic; they are not limited to natural resource management nor are they likely to be transitory or cosmetic.

The effectiveness of recreation planning is impacted by these changes. Planning, for example, in a stable and predictable environment is very different than planning in a turbulent and uncertain one, even though the ultimate goal of planning—to ensure a desired future arrives—is the same. Thus, in this chapter, we elaborate on these changes and suggest their implications for the conduct of recreation planning: we identify some of the key features of these fundamental changes in the social, political, and economic context within which contemporary planning and management must operate. Six key areas are identified: (1) the decisionmaking environment, (2) technology, (3) population growth and change, (4) public values, (5) economic restructuring, and (6) governance. For each of these, a brief description of the underlying nature of changes is provided along with a short outline of some of the key implications of those changes for planners and managers.

Planning in a stable and predictable environment is very different than planning in a turbulent and uncertain one.

Decisionmaking Environment

A hallmark of natural resource planning and management in past years was the high level of discretion available to, and exercised by, agency personnel. In the case of the USDA Forest Service, the core legislation upon which the agency operated—the 1960 Multiple Use-Sustained Yield Act—was steeped in such implicit discretion; during one of the many legal challenges facing the agency, a federal judge observed that the act "breathes discretion at every pore" (cited in Wondolleck 1988). However, such discretion derived from a widespread belief that most of the problems confronting agencies were technical or scientific in nature and that the requisite skills and knowledge to resolve those problems satisfactorily were possessed by a professionally trained agency staff. Because the problems were of a technical or scientific character, their satisfactory resolution[1] also was dependent upon the application of a particular set of knowledge and skills, which were largely possessed only by those with the appropriate type of education and experience. Moreover, decisionmaking was marked by a burden of proof argument in which planned actions were overturned or halted only upon emerging evidence that their effects were not those intended.

Today, these fundamental dimensions of the decisionmaking environment have been dramatically recast. Management discretion has been significantly replaced by an increasing reliance upon an array of regulatory mechanisms, prescriptive legislation, and oversight organizations. Jasanoff (1990) has provided considerable detail regarding the forces that have led to such a change, but at the core lies an increasing level of distrust regarding organizational decisionmaking by both oversight agencies and the wider public. As a result, there is growing direction from legislatively-prescribed mechanisms and the imposition of administrative regulations that require external oversight by regulatory bodies such as the National Marine Fisheries Service or the U.S. Fish and Wildlife Service.

In addition to the impact of these external legal strictures, there is also an increasingly prevalent reliance on the precautionary principle. Although this principle has been defined various ways, its manifestation in a land management planning context has largely been one in which human interventions are treated as likely

---

[1] In this text, we use the term "resolution" or "resolve" deliberately, and to mean that an agreement has been reached on how to deal with a problem. In this sense, resolutions of problems are only temporary as new contexts raise old questions over and over. We do not use it to mean that a problem has been solved.

sources of adverse impacts; it imposes a requirement that in the presence of uncertainty, extreme caution be exercised in any intervention (Cooney and Dickson 2005). Because of an increasing recognition of the limits of contemporary science in efforts to manage at larger spatial and longer time scales and of the need to look at secondary and tertiary effects of any action, the ability to foresee such adverse consequences is almost always problematic. The practical effect of the precautionary principle then often becomes one that restricts interventions or experimentation until such time that "enough" is known. Coupled with the restrictive legal environment, the ideology of the precautionary principle has created a situation in which risk-aversion has become the norm, and maintenance of the status quo often dominates decisionmaking (even though the concept of a "no action" alternative is not without a host of its own risks, consequences, and impacts).

With regard to recreation planning and management, decisions about development of overnight facilities, access systems (e.g., trails, roads, and bridges) and other supporting tourism facilities often raise questions concerning possible impacts on endangered species habitat or aquatic and riparian environments. Often, the inclination is to avoid undertaking any action that **might** result in any adverse impact. Either actively or passively discouraging recreation use in riparian zones, for example, is justified on the grounds that such restrictions effectively preserve key habitat, even if evidence of any adverse impacts is lacking. In sum, decisionmaking has become increasingly conservative, reactive, and resistant to change; protection and maintenance of the status quo prevails. The principal impact of these changes in decisionmaking has been to foster a conservative, risk-averse environment that emphasizes compliance with environmental procedures. The use of adaptive management regimes is also adversely impacted, as the notion of experimentation may be antithetical to the precautionary principle.

Technology

The impact of technology on planning in general, and on recreation and tourism planning reveals itself in two ways. First, there continue to be major changes in the technology of recreation and tourism activities. There have been a host of developments in off-road vehicles, global positioning systems, cell phones, recreational equipment, clothing and materials, and other apparatus that facilitate recreational use (e.g., jet skis). Such developments are driven largely by changes in technological capacity and links between these changes and market demand. Moreover, land managers and planners often find themselves reacting to the latest development or fad, and the associated adverse impacts on other users or the environment occur with little in the way of forethought or preplanning. Yet, it also needs to be understood that technology has always been present, and changes in it have always had impacts on the types, levels, and distribution of recreation use; that is, this is not simply a contemporary phenomenon. Whether we are talking about the advent of outboard motors, aluminum-frame backpacks, dehydrated foods, or the automobile, the character and level of recreation use facing planners and managers has long been the product of technological change.

Complicating the response to technological innovation has been an apparent acceleration in technological development. Old technologies are not those that are a decade or so old, they may be only a year or two old. The implication here is that it has become extremely difficult for agencies to maintain a technological awareness and understand the effects of new technology on the type and distribution of demand for recreation.

Some technologies, such as GPS, have resulted in new recreation activities on wildlands, such as geocaching.

Technology also has dramatically affected the provision of information. The advent of global positioning system (GPS) and the array of remote and satellite imagery, for instance, have changed forever the ways in which resource management information is compiled, displayed, and used. The opportunities for the rapid and accurate display of information about resource systems and different management actions have greatly enhanced the ability of resource managers to understand how an action might relate to different resources, uses, and values. In addition, some technologies, such as GPS, have resulted in new recreation activities on wildlands, such as geocaching, where a "treasure" is hidden and its locational coordinates are broadcast over the Internet. Users with GPS units then attempt to find the treasure, and if they do, leave a small note or prize for the next finder.

However, this explosion in information technology is not limited to the resource management community. The World Wide Web and its host of powerful search engines have dramatically recast the way in which potential recreationists obtain information about destinations and opportunities. Although data are lacking, it seems clear that increasingly, recreationists are able to obtain information with little or no direct contact with public resource management agencies. For example, Whitmore et al. (2005) reported that over 8 percent of the visitors to the Bob Marshall Wilderness in Montana used Internet information sources to plan their visit. The extent to which such information is consistent with rules and regulations, organizational objectives, or other management considerations is problematic. Yet, such use likely will become even more of a factor in the future.

Although data again are lacking, we can identify some of the consequences of this phenomenon of the growth and utilization of information technology. It has the potential of increasing both the levels and diversity of recreational demand that public lands must face. It could also have impacts on the spatial and temporal distribution of recreation use, as information about opportunities and access become widely available. Such shifts, as noted above, have the potential for a variety of management problems; increased levels of use, conflicts among recreation uses, and conflicts with or impacts upon, other resource uses. In turn, these latter issues could increase the level of impact on agencies in terms of law enforcement, supervision, cleanup, and maintenance. Moreover, because the quality and accuracy of information that recreationists and tourists obtain on the Web cannot be accurately judged, the potential for unrealistic or misplaced expectations could be great. Images of sites and landscapes conjured up by Web sites may differ in their accuracy or realism, giving rise to expectations that may or may not be consistent with the current management regime or conditions. But, given the proliferation of such data and the number of sources from which it is obtained, it will be challenging for agency personnel to monitor, let alone clarify or correct it. As a consequence, there could be increasing numbers of recreationists and tourists who bring expectations and demands to public lands that are inaccurate or misplaced.

Population Growth and Change

Since the end of World War II, the U.S. population has increased by about 50 million people every 20 years; according to the U.S. census today, it stands at more than 300 million. Yet, from a recreation and tourism planning perspective, it is less the total change in population that is of interest than it is the composition and distribution of that population. Although there has been much discussion about reducing population growth to a "replacement level," and the natural increase (births minus deaths) has slowed, this will not occur for many years. However, the dynamics of population growth and change result in a number of significant consequences for recreation and tourism planners.

First, although the Nation's total population growth has slowed, there have been significant shifts in the distribution of the population, driven by large-scale and long-lasting patterns of migration. The result is some sectors of the country, notably the Western States, have been marked by substantial population growth. Some of the internal migration is fed by the search for employment, but amenity values remain a major factor (Beale and Johnson 1998, McGranahan 1999). In

Ravalli County of western Montana, 80 to 90 percent of its total population growth since the late 1970s is accounted for by immigration. Throughout the Western United States, counties that have relatively large proportions of public lands and, in particular, national parks and wildernesses, have seen growth rates that exceed regional averages, as many economically "footloose" households have chosen to live in amenity-rich areas. Such growth is also fostered by the types of changes in information technology discussed earlier that permit certain employment sectors to telecommute. And, there may be conflicting views of nature and land management between the oldtimers and newcomers (Fortmann and Kusel 1991, Graber 1974).

Second, the U.S. population is increasingly older; by 2030, it is estimated that 20 percent of the Nation's population will exceed age 65 (He et al. 2005). The fastest growing age category is the 85 and older, according to the U.S. census. And, although at one time, increasing age was clearly associated with declining participation rates in almost all recreation activities, this is much less true now. People now in their retirement years come from an age cohort where recreation was an integral part of their lifestyle, and many people retain their participation patterns or switch to allied activities (e.g., from running to walking, backpacking to day hiking). Increasing numbers of persons in postretirement also might lead to an extended use season, from the traditional emphasis on the Memorial Day to Labor Day period to year round. Moreover, the changes in leisure and outdoor recreation technology noted earlier likely enable these individuals to participate longer than before. Even when these individuals no longer participate in recreation at their former rates, or at all, they might still remain engaged in recreation and tourism planning processes, given the long-term importance of the activity in their lives or of the places in which those activities were undertaken. As a consequence, the knowledge, experiences, and expectations of a population no longer active onsite will remain issues with which managers must deal.

Third, the traditional rural to urban migration pattern has reversed itself in many parts of the West. In the early 1990s, nearly all counties in the Pacific Northwest experienced this pattern, which was particularly dramatic in counties containing natural resource based amenities, such as national parks, designated wilderness, and wild and scenic rivers (Rudzitis and Johansen 1989, Troy 1998). Although the current pattern of migration is limited to urban proximate counties, amenity resources—in addition to land prices—are probably largely responsible for continued population growth in these places (McCool and Kruger 2003).

Fourth, the Nation is increasingly ethnically diverse (USDC Bureau of the Census 2002); in some regions of the country, such as the Southwest, non-Caucasians now account for a majority of the population. This presents challenges across a variety of sectors—education, health care—and for the provision of outdoor recreation and tourism services. Cultural beliefs and norms mean that new demands and expectations will be increasingly brought to bear on the provision of these services. Different languages, or even limited proficiency in English, will challenge communication programs both onsite as well as in such venues as public involvement efforts. The ability to gain public understanding and support for a variety of programs, both in recreation/tourism and other arenas, such as biodiversity conservation, might prove challenging. Finally, understanding the meaning and importance of outdoor engagements—for subsistence, for leisure, for spiritual purposes—will often prove difficult for managers from a Caucasian, Anglo perspective.

The effect of population growth and change has been to dramatically increase demand for recreational opportunities on public lands, in particular in those places containing publicly administered amenity resources. Places that once had few visitors now have many. This increased demand may conflict with established patterns of resource commodity production, leading to competing views of what products public lands provide. Another effect has been to diversify recreational demand. Older individuals and those with different ethnic background may engage in different activities. The mode of their engagement in recreational activities may differ. The tourism industry itself may find a need to adapt to changing age structures and preferences resulting from the aging process, such as building more lodges and designing activities that meet the preferences of older Americans.

The effect of population growth and change has been to dramatically increase demand for recreational opportunities on public lands.

Public Values

The structural changes in population discussed above have been accompanied by equally telling shifts in public attitudes and values with respect to the environment and the management of public lands. Generally, not only have recreation participation rates remained high, but public concern with questions of environmental quality and protection have gained support (however, whether a causal link exists between these factors is not known). National surveys of public values about the environment provide evidence that environmental issues still attract citizen interest among a wide range of political priorities. For example, Steel and Weber (2003) reported that in a national survey, over 60 percent of respondents considered themselves to be at least "moderately informed" about the concept of ecosystem management as applied to public land management. Among these respondents, the basis of support for ecosystem management tended to focus on the value of the framework for thinking about the environment in holistic rather than a single resource basis, as a means of protecting endangered species while ensuring certain commodity values, and for enhancing the long-term health of the public lands. Other surveys suggest that a host of symbolic dimensions of environmental management remain important; spiritual values, scientific inquiry, cultural purposes, and the like (e.g., Manning et al. 1999, Steel et al. 1994).

However, the public support for recreation and tourism uses of the environment can conflict with public preferences and backing for the maintenance of habitat for threatened and endangered species, biodiversity conservation, or other conservation purposes. The view of recreation as environmentally benign may be challenged in these conflict situations. For example, proposals for large-scale ski resorts using public lands for ski runs are routinely criticized for their impact on biophysical conditions and processes.

Nonetheless, survey data such as these clearly indicate that environmental management remains a salient public issue. Moreover, the pluralistic nature of our Nation suggests that the option for managing for one set of values (e.g., recreation and tourism) versus some other set (e.g., environmental protection) as an "either-or" matter is not a politically viable choice; both are sought and considered important. Thus, managers must seek frameworks that respond to these pluralistic—and often conflicting—demands in a manner that makes it possible to be responsive to both.

Economic Restructuring

Recent decades have witnessed a major restructuring of the U.S. economy. A variety of factors account for this change, some global, some national, others local. Economists give particular attention to the notion of "uncoupling"; that is, a fundamental change in the relationship between key components of the economy. First, there has been an uncoupling of the primary products economy, such as timber, from the industrial economy. In short, the industrial economy has disconnected itself from its dependence upon primary products, a phenomenon driven largely by technology. Thus, for example, alternative products have replaced traditional siding and flooring. Second, there has been an uncoupling of production in the industrial economy from industrial employment; that is, output and efficiency in the industrial sector have grown while employment in that sector has declined (Carroll and

Blatner 1994, Drucker 1986). Again, this largely stems from productivity gains owing to technology; mills that once required 100 people to run a shift can now do so with 20.

Third, there has also been a significant shift in the underlying complexity of our economic system; economic relations and interdependencies are increasingly complex and difficult to understand and manipulate. This shift flows from a variety of national and international policies and programs (e.g., North America Free Trade Agreement), from the growing globalization and internationalization of commercial activity, and from technological change. The seemingly simple maxim to "buy American" holds little meaning when Chevrolets[2] are built in Mexico and Canada and Toyotas are assembled in Ohio. And, finally, the economies of small, rural communities in the West have largely been uncoupled from resource commodity production and processing. Many communities have lost their sawmills, grain storage, and mining dependencies; some have replaced these with a service- and retirement-based economy. In some communities, retirement income (annuities, social security, and so on) make up 20 percent or more of the personal income.

The Bureau of Economic Analysis keeps track of such statistics. A couple of examples illustrate the importance of this source of income. In the Missoula, Montana, Economic Region, for example, such transfer payments totaled about 17 percent of the total personal income in 2003, but were increasing at the rate of 5.4 percent per year during the previous decade. The Bend, Oregon, economic region has a similar proportion, but the rate of increase is much higher at 8.3 percent per year. If one adds in dividends, interest, and rent as a source of income, then the proportion of personal income in both areas owing to nonlabor income sources rises to 38 percent and more (USDC Bureau of Economic Analysis 2006).

Such changes impact natural resource and recreation management in many ways. The increasing emphasis and concern with efficiency, cost-reduction, and profit margins has seen a major shift in the locus of U.S. timber production, moving from the Pacific Northwest region to the Southeast and its short-term-rotation pine forests. Combined with gains in technological efficiency, the sum has been a significant economic impact in many rural communities of the region, as the long-term source of economic well-being and jobs have disappeared. These changes and

---

[2] The use of trade or firm names in this publication is for reader information and does not imply endorsement by the U.S. Department of Agriculture of any product or service.

others involving legal challenges, were responsible, in large part, for the 1993 Forest Conference in Portland, Oregon, where President Clinton sought to find a strategy for resolving the gridlock that gripped forest management in the region.

The decline in timber production in the Northwest has had two important impacts on recreation and tourism. First, the loss of a once-prosperous economic base has led many rural communities to seek alternative means of sustaining themselves; recreation and tourism represent one potential vector of economic development. As a result, there has been a growth in private sector and commercial efforts to provide an array of recreation services, with public lands providing the resources required for those services. However, two major challenges face both communities and public land managers. First, how can communities exploit the natural capital located on public land without unacceptably altering the quality of the very resources upon which the burgeoning recreation/tourism industry ultimately depends? In some cases, proposals to increase the economic reliance of communities on tourism have been met with stiff opposition, both on environmental and economic grounds. Second, what is the capacity of these communities to effectively organize and deliver an array of recreation and tourism services in terms of the needed financial and social capital? With regard to both questions, there is a need for frameworks that enable public and private planners to more effectively define the nature, distribution, and scope of recreation and tourism demand and supply.

The second impact of the decline in timber harvesting has been a loss of capacity of management programs within the federal resource agencies. For many years, timber management budgets helped subsidize activities within other resource programs, including recreation and wildlife. With the decline of the timber industry, there has been a parallel decline in agency timber management programs and diminishing budgets felt in those programs once supported by timber dollars. Coupled with impacts on recreation staff, the sum effect has been a major decline in the extent and quality of recreation management programs including direct provision of opportunities and loss of capacity to assess impacts to public lands from private tourism development.

Governance

The question of how a society organizes itself to achieve a variety of purposes has long preoccupied many observers. In recent years, this issue has gained increasing attention and is as true for natural resource management as it is for any other

> **There has been a growth in private sector and commercial efforts to provide an array of recreation services, with public lands providing the resources required for those services.**

sector. At the broadest level, it involves a fundamental tension between a conception of governance grounded in a "federalist" model, in which responsibilities are embodied in a centralized structure (e.g., the federal government) as opposed to one often described as a "Jeffersonian" model, in which responsibilities and governance are devolved to local authorities. In the United States today, elements of both are found. However, a growing sense of dissatisfaction and frustration with "traditional" government suggests the search for more effective, efficient, and equitable structures and processes continues.

Although this is sometimes cast as a politically partisan issue, it is broader than that. For example, during the Clinton administration, much attention focused on the recommendations and ideas contained in the book *Reinventing Government: How the Entrepreneurial Spirit Is Transforming the Public Sector* (Osborne and Gaebler 1992). In August, 2004, an Executive Order signed by President Bush called for particular attention on the part of federal natural resource agencies to cooperative and collaborative relations with public and private interests at the local level in conservation planning. In the forestry sector, O'Toole's book *Reforming the Forest Service* (1988) called for the devolution of many responsibilities to states, local government, and the private sector. In recent years, burgeoning interest in alternative models of governance have gained increased attention—for example, the increased attention given to a host of collaborative management approaches (Wondolleck and Yaffee 2000) and experiments in comanagement (e.g., between existing public authorities and Native Americans).

In response, some on-the-ground projects have appeared (e.g., the Quincy Library Group in northern California); former Oregon Governor John Kitzhaber has established a policy research center to consider alternative institutional structures and processes. These proposals, and many others, reflect widespread dissatisfaction with the top-down, command and control models of planning that have typified natural resource management agencies. The continuing impact of "not in my backyard" concerns reflects a sense of frustration and powerlessness on the part of many citizens about government actions that ignore local concerns with place. In some cases, these frustrations have triggered local political actions, often in the form of so-called "friends of" groups that attempt to exert political influence upon the actions of a government seen as disconnected and unconcerned with local issues.

In sum, these and other related movements reflect the continuing search for more effective instruments of governance. They also reveal an evolving conception about traditional approaches to natural resource planning. For example, there is a growing sense that the traditional view of planning as a technical enterprise (the so-called "social reform" model; see Friedmann 1987) needs to be augmented by a "social learning" model, which conceives of planning as both a technical **and** sociopolitical endeavor. Again, the growing interest in a variety of collaborative approaches to planning reflects this concern. It is also driven and sustained by statutory and policy mandates (e.g., National Environmental Policy Act 1969) that give citizens increased roles and responsibilities in natural resource decisionmaking; this has significantly altered the relation between citizen and natural resource organizations and the trend likely will extend citizen influence even further.

One specific dimension of the contemporary political scene involves efforts to reduce government in general and the federal government in particular. Some of the authority and responsibility has been assigned to various local governments (states, counties, and municipalities), whereas others are seen as more appropriately met by the private sector. Coupled with the types of fundamental economic restructuring described earlier, one major impact has been the downsizing of personnel. For example, personnel dropped by about 50 percent between 1994 and 2004 in the Pacific Northwest Region (Region 6, Oregon, Washington, and Alaska) of the Forest Service. This has had three major impacts in natural resource management. First, the reduction in full-time professional staff has not been accompanied by any significant reduction in responsibilities and requirements. Thus, individual employees typically find themselves handling more than one full-time position. This horizontal job-loading has led to a situation with the consequence that the time, attention, and energy devoted to any one responsibility, such as recreation management, increasingly are diminished and diluted.

Second, internal rules of seniority and personnel management in federal organizations have led to a situation in which, as various downsizing measures are taken, staff in fields such as silviculture or engineering find themselves reassigned to responsibilities for which they might be poorly equipped to meet or for which they have little interest. Thus, people lacking the educational background, on-the-ground experience and training, and sometimes the interest to proactively manage the resources assigned to them, fill some recreation staff positions.

Third, as noted in the discussion of economic restructuring, political, economic, and policy pressures have resulted in increased attention to alternative sources of economic support for local communities. Chief among these have been efforts to enhance these communities as venues for recreation and tourism and for the development of local capacity to offer recreation and tourism services. Again, coupled with a declining federal workforce and pressures to devolve formerly federal responsibilities to other governmental levels or the private sector, the sum effect has been to reduce the federal presence in the planning, provision, and management of recreation and tourism. For example, many Forest Service campgrounds in the Northwest are now managed by private firms, leaving the public without any direct contact with federal rangers.

The ultimate effect of these changes is substantial and complex. Precisely when there is significant social and political pressure to rely on public lands as a source of recreation and tourism development opportunities, the agencies are losing their organizational capital, as measured in both numbers and breadth of skill set, to provide for those opportunities. The increasing pressures for more collaborative models of decisionmaking are counter-balanced by a loss of personnel to do the collaboration. The growing level and diversity of demand for recreation and tourism opportunities collides with reduced administrative discretion to provide those opportunities. Responding to changing public values and preferences for the outputs of public land management clashes with a growing tendency to view recreation management in highly reductionistic ways. These clashes have led to a greater reliance on private contractors, but there are significant questions about the capacity of contractors to carry out the complex, and often changing, responsibilities assigned to public land agencies.

The growing level and diversity of demand for recreation and tourism opportunities collides with reduced administrative discretion to provide those opportunities.

What Do These Changes Mean for Recreation Planning?

Planning is conducted by government agencies and their employees. Each of these agencies has a distinctive culture, which not only socializes employees into what is important to attend to (e.g., agency norms, values, positions) but which also carries with it certain assumptions—often implicit—about the character of its external environment, the appropriateness of planning processes to the issues with which it is confronted, and the context within which it is situated. Given the complexity, dimensionality, and pace of external change, there are a number of implications for the organizations that conduct planning for recreation on public lands.

First, the implicit assumptions that the organization carries about its external environment—the expectations its constituencies hold, the processes civil society engages to protect important values, the saliency of the organization to wider society—are challenged. Although these implicit assumptions are critical in day-to-day operations of the organization, they also may lead to increasing irrelevancy in a time of change and uncertainty. Thus, the same assumptions about the environment that have led to an organization's success in the past may also be responsible for conflict with its constituencies in the future. What this suggests for planning agencies is a need for sensing mechanisms to determine what changes are occurring and why, so the organization can become as adaptable as the management of public lands it wishes to implement. The acceptability of management actions and uses is subject to constant change: what once was acceptable is no longer (e.g., snow-mobiling in Yellowstone National Park). How do agencies sense these changes in their external environment? How do they organize themselves to learn about these changes and address them?

Second, the character of the planning problem has shifted (see next section), indeed jumped, from the tame—typified by social agreement on goals and agreement among scientists on cause-effect relationships—to the messy situations where disagreement on both exists. The implication for planning agencies is that the processes and approaches to problems that once were adequate are no longer. Typical rational-comprehensive planning, relying on science and driven by expertise, exacerbate rather than resolve recreation issues. The challenge for organizations is to find or develop, when needed, frameworks that will be responsive and effective in this changed planning situation.

A third major implication is that development of a variety of interlocked contextual elements challenges the capacity of public land recreation agencies to respond to the growing complexity of planning issues. Although any one of the trends or driving forces mentioned earlier would present a formidable challenge itself, the synergistic quality of them acting together—colliding and reinforcing as they do—requires thoughtful, defendable, and trackable responses to planning issues. It is as if the contemporary planner must now follow a twisting, narrow pathway, bounded by precipices in the search for resolutions to a growing number of issues. A suitable framework provides the guide for navigating this challenging, and often unforgiving, pathway.

Finally, as we note in the next section, there are a variety of interlocked issues confronting public land recreation planners (Allen and Gould 1986). One issue cannot necessarily be resolved without the others being addressed. Although traditional expert-driven planning processes are still necessary, they are no longer adequate for resolution of these issues.

Contemporary Recreation and Tourism Development Planning Issues

This context, as turbulent, contentious, and complex as it is, sets the stage for a number of issues concerning recreation and tourism development on public lands. These issues, many of which have dogged land management agencies for decades, require a framework to structure thinking, to help planners "work through" them, and to assist in identifying appropriate responses and implementation strategies.

We have identified some of these issues below. We have framed the issue as a question, and then provided a brief description. Our framing of these issues is necessarily abstract, but each issue is played out at a local (park, forest or district) level, and so the specifics differ from one place to another. This local context is critical to framing the issue at that level—the scale at which appropriate responses will be made.

What are the interactions between recreation and other uses of public lands?

- Recreation on public lands frequently occurs within the context of other uses, both utilitarian, such as timber harvesting, grazing, habitat protection, and symbolic, such as visual quality, and spiritual meanings. How recreation is managed affects the ability of public lands to produce or preserve these other uses, and conversely, management for these other values influences what opportunities, where, and how many exist for recreation. In allocating lands to various uses, planners need to understand what tradeoffs, costs, and consequences result from different proposed allocation decisions.

Under what conditions can recreational use be limited, and what criteria would be needed to make visitor use allocation decisions?

- In certain situations, managers may feel that recreation use must be limited to a certain number of people during a specific period. Such use limits have often been implemented on western whitewater rivers. Use limits are generally implemented when there have been clear threats to the biophysical or experiential component of a particular setting. When use limits are imposed and demand is above what the limit allows, use must be rationed and allocated. By allocation, we mean dividing up the total use among commercial outfitted groups and private visitor groups, a common practice in river situations. Rationing is the process for determining the specific individuals that are permitted to enter the setting.

What are the regional effects of site-level decisions?

- Recreation sites, and larger areas, such as national parks, exist within a complex web of interacting supply-and-demand processes. Managers acting to protect or enhance the recreation attributes or tourism opportunities at one site may implement a series of actions that restricts people or their behavior, but in reality, the problem pops up someplace else. For example, acting to limit use on one site may displace use to other sites because at least some users can no longer access the original site. In some situations, the organizational capacity to deal with increased use and impact may be very limited on the sites now attracting the displaced users.

How can allocations of use opportunities between guided and nonguided publics be made?

- Limiting recreational use will often require that limits also be placed on the number of "service days" of use allowed for guided use and on the number of visitor days of use allowed for the nonguided public. This decision is akin to cutting a highly desirable pie into two slices (sometimes more, depending upon agency and outfitting policy). Criteria are needed to determine what proportion of use should be guided and nonguided. Within this decision there are also decisions to allot use to individual guides and outfitters and to ration use among other visitors, assuming demand is above the allocated use. Outfitters generally ration use based on price, whereas for nonguided visitors, rationing may be based on a waiting line, reservation, random drawing, or a combination of techniques.

How can decisionmakers better link settings, experiences, and uses?

- In a sense, managers produce opportunities for people to experience certain sociopsychological outcomes. These opportunities are composed of attributes; combinations of attributes lead to the notion of setting. Attributes are things like rules, regulations, visitor-use density, visitor types, and amount and type of modification of the natural environment. Combinations of attributes lead to settings that have certain similarities; such settings can be classified. However, the link between setting attributes and the sociopsychological outcomes is anything but clear. Indeed, settings represent opportunities in the sense that they facilitate one type of sociopsychological outcome over another, but do not ensure that a particular outcome actually occurs. The actual production of the outcome remains with the visitor. A major challenge, however, is to increase our understanding of how settings, experiences (the package of sociopsychological outcomes produced by the visitor), and other uses are linked. Increasing our understanding would allow more efficient and mindful allocation of opportunities to settings.

What is the role of tourism as a component of a community's economy?

- Shifts in economic restructuring have increased not only the economic importance of tourism in Western U.S. economics but also have changed relationships between communities and adjacent public lands. As employment and revenue from traditional resource commodity processing has dropped, many communities have turned to tourism as a tool to maintain their economic and social vitality. For many of these communities, however, the product sought by nonresident visitors is located on publicly administered lands, and even may be found in congressionally designated areas such as wilderness, wild and scenic rivers, national parks. Other nondesignated lands managed by the Forest Service or Bureau of Land Management may also contain settings for recreation that are popular with nonresidents. Understanding what economic role tourism may hold in a community is difficult because many businesses in the tourism sector also appeal to residents, such as restaurants, service stations, and lodging. Sorting out what is attributable to tourism is difficult.

How do changes in the amount, location, and character of the human population impact formulation of policy?

- The Western United States has experienced dramatic population changes over the last 15 years. These changes have generally resulted from significant in-migration, particularly to rural areas and more specifically into the wildland-urban interface. Such population growth has brought generally younger, less affluent individuals into these areas, but individuals also with a different distribution of intellectual skills, social preferences, and activism than the current residents. This population growth also accompanies structural shifts in regional economies, generally from manufacturing, natural-resource-dependent economies to service- and amenity-dependent economies. Such population growth is relatively widespread in counties with a large proportion of land managed by the federal government; about 94 percent of the counties in the United States with more than 30 percent of their land base in federal stewardship saw significant population growth in the 1990s.

What public land recreation opportunities should be commercialized and privatized?

- With decreasing budgets and more conservative political philosophies, managers are under more pressure to commercialize recreation opportunities on public lands. Such commercialization and any accompanying privatization would increase the costs to the recreating public, raise expectations of the quality of opportunity to be provided, and increase revenues to management. But which recreation opportunities should be commercialized? What criteria would be used to make this decision?

What public lands should be allocated to what types of recreational opportunities?

- As the population grows, and as preferences for recreation in wildland environments strengthens, the demands on these environments as places to enjoy recreation will increase. In many cases, allocation of land to one use will preclude other recreational uses from occurring there. How will a manager or planner decide what lands should be allocated to what uses and opportunities? What criteria and standards will be useful in making this decision? What claims to lands are most effective?

Chapter 3: An Overview of Recreation and Tourism Frameworks

What Is a Framework?

The needs identified in chapter 1 and the driving forces, trends, and issues presented in chapter 2 combine to accelerate the need for frameworks to structure decisions about provision of recreation and tourism development opportunities on public lands. Such frameworks have existed for the last quarter century or so, and have had varying degrees of "success" in application and resolution of issues confronting public land management. The fundamental purpose of this paper, as we noted earlier, is to provide managers with a primer on these frameworks. In this chapter, we provide a brief overview of the set of frameworks that are currently available. By "framework," we mean a process that involves a sequence of steps that leads managers and planners to explicate the particular issue. A "framework" in this sense does not necessarily lead to formulation of "the" answer to an issue, but provides the conceptual basis through which the issue may be successfully resolved.

A limited number of frameworks exist, and many have similar characteristics, but may have been developed in specific policy and administrative contexts that influence the particular elements or components involved. We note that several overviews and comparative analyses of recreation and tourism frameworks exist (Manning 2004, Moore et al. 2003, Nilsen and Tayler 1997). Each is helpful in familiarizing the reader with these frameworks; however, they are not directed toward understanding a framework's usefulness in addressing the variety of issues confronting managers nor do they discuss the principal concepts and premises upon which these frameworks are built. Finally, such reviews do not necessarily provide the type of information managers would need to make decisions about what framework to use in a particular set of circumstances.

Not all recreation frameworks are suitable for all issues confronting public land recreation. And there may yet be issues for which no suitable framework exists. Nevertheless, decisionmakers must evaluate the suitability of a framework for a specific issue. But what would guide this evaluation? We suggest use of five criteria to assess the suitability of a framework for resolving issues of public land recreation management:

A primary consideration is the **saliency** of the framework to the particular problem in a specific planning situation. Not all frameworks were designed to address all issues confronting public land recreation planners. Indeed, as shown in

Not all recreation frameworks are suitable for all issues confronting public land recreation.

chapter 2, a wide range of issues exist. Therefore, as a first step, a framework should provide a process for working through the specific issue confronting managers. In particular, the framework should help clarify the issue and frame it appropriately.

The next set of criteria are adapted from Brewer (1973). The framework should be conceptually sound, based on the most current and appropriate science and theory. In this sense, use of the framework should be relatively easy to defend to one's peers. Major concepts underlie the principal frameworks reviewed here, and we present brief descriptions of each.

The framework should also meet certain technical criteria and be easily translated into practice. For example, one would want to know what types of knowledge, skills, and abilities are needed for implementation. The organization would want to know what commitments are being made once implemented, and how the organizational structure might be affected. One would want to know if the organization has the technical capacity to implement the framework; in addition, several of the frameworks described have been implemented with a substantial public engagement component. Does the agency have the technical public facilitation skills or can it acquire those?

The framework must meet an ethical criterion as well, that is, it should identify the distributional consequences of a decision. Public land management is about allocating the flow of benefits, ideally in a manner that such benefits are optimized. But such benefits do not come without some cost, both financial and social. So, what groups or values may benefit from a particular decision? Who might be paying the cost, or find access restricted or impacted? A framework should help a manager work through these questions.

Finally, the framework must be pragmatic, that is, it must be both efficient (getting the biggest bang for the buck) and it must be effective (it helps achieve larger goals, such as optimizing the flow of benefits from public lands). This is an important criterion because the framework should help decisionmakers allocate scarce financial and personnel resources to important and salient tasks.

What Frameworks Are in the Planner's Toolbox?

The primer found in chapter 4 is arranged around the most fundamental frameworks that have been identified in the recreation/tourism literature and that have enough record of application that they can be assessed. We order this discussion historically, that is, we begin with a discussion of recreation carrying capacity, a frequently cited approach to managing recreation issues, and then progress to those developed more recently. In this discussion, we provide an overview of the framework, the rationale for why it developed, the key concepts important for application and implementation, and assess experience in real world application.

A limited number of frameworks exist to assist public land recreation managers to address 21st century public land recreation management issues. In general, there are four genres of recreation planning frameworks available:

- Recreation Carrying Capacity
- Recreation Opportunity Spectrum (ROS)
- Limits of Acceptable Change (LAC), including Visitor Experience and Resource Protection
- Benefits-Based Management

These frameworks represent an evolution in not only how recreation issues on public lands are addressed but also in how they are framed. In a very real sense, they represent a critique or dissatisfaction with prior approaches to recreation planning. Table 1 also shows the principal question addressed by each of the frameworks we have included here. For the ROS and LAC framework, several variants and derivative adaptations have been developed (although the Visitor Impact Management framework was developed independently, it contains similar concepts, and thus is considered a variant of LAC). Although some of these frameworks were developed relatively independently, several address a similar principal question, and similar concepts and premises underlie several. Each framework, however, serves public land recreation managers in different ways and varies in its suitability in addressing current and anticipated issues.

For nearly all the frameworks, there is considerable case-to-case variance in how they have been implemented, particularly with respect to public engagement and completeness. For example, LAC makes no explicit mention of a public engagement step, but in its initial application (and in many others) public engagement was a critical component. In others, there was little public engagement.

Conditions Needed to Implement a Recreation Planning Framework

Of course the frameworks listed in table 1 can only be implemented if a set of conditions are present in the agency considering using a framework. These are

Table 1—An inventory of existing frameworks available for recreation planning issues on public lands

Framework	Variants/derivates	Principal question	Key references
Recreation Opportunity Spectrum	Recreation Opportunity Spectrum, 1980s Tourism Opportunity Spectrum, 1990s Water Recreation Opportunity Spectrum, 2000s	What settings exist and what should be provided?	Clark and Stankey 1979, Dawson 2001, Driver and Brown 1978, Haas et al. 2004
Limits of Acceptable Change	Limits of Acceptable Change, 1980s Visitor Impact Management, 1980s Visitor Experience and Resource Protection, 1990s Tourism Optimization and Management Model, 1990s	How much change from natural conditions is acceptable?	Graefe et al. 1990, Hof and Lime 1997, Manidis Roberts 1997 Stankey et al. 1985
The Benefits Based Management, 1990s		What experiences should be provided?	Driver and Bruns 1999
Carrying (Visitor) Capacity, 1960s + Social Biophysical Facility	Visitor capacity, 2000s	How many is too many?	Lime and Stankey 1971 Haas 2002
Placed based, 2000s[a]		What meanings are attached to this place?	Kruger and Jakes 2003

[a] Not discussed here.

briefly discussed below, but a more extensive discussion of requirements is developed in the primer chapter. Each of the conditions below will be required to varying degrees for each of the frameworks.

The agency must have the **organizational will** to implement the framework in full. Several of the frameworks listed in table 1 consist of a sequence of steps, elements or components. Each of these is essential to successful completion of the framework, and thus resolution of the underlying problem. Managers often ask for shortcuts to using the framework; what steps can be dropped or indicators and standards borrowed from other areas and so on. Although this might seem a good way to cut costs in the short term, planning frameworks are not about the short term—they are about learning, thinking about the future, engaging the public, and strategic analysis. Each step or element is included for a specific reason; dropping any out is counter to these values of planning. Thus, the organization most importantly must have the determination to complete the process.

Related to this condition is that the personnel involved cannot be rushed, careless, or distracted. They must have the time and resources to complete a planning process competently. This would require the organization to develop and make available the time needed to work through the challenges of a recreation issue.

Second, the organization needs the **technical capacity** to conduct the planning processes. By this, we mean the organization needs the personnel with the appropriate skills, some technical, some in public meeting facilitation depending on the approach used. This means the organization must not only seek out trained individuals, but also engage in in-service training and continuing education to maintain an up-to-date work force.

Third, the process must be **inclusive** of differing values and systems of knowledge. Many decisions in recreation management are value judgments (Krumpe and McCool 1997) and thus a full discussion of the values involved is essential to addressing recreation management problems. This can only be done with inclusive public engagement processes because technical planners cannot be expected to equitably represent every value system. In addition, there must be recognition that different forms of knowledge (e.g., experiential, scientific) are not only legitimate ways of knowing but each contributes constructively at different points in a planning process.

Fourth, the process must be **open and deliberative**, with opportunities to express, challenge, and debate different assumptions (among managers, scientists, and members of the public) underlying proposed actions and goals. The planning process must therefore secure safe and accessible venues, ones that symbolize equality of access and so on. This quality is as important for purely technical planning processes, (as it assures different viewpoints, theoretical perspectives, and data quality and saliency issues are brought out) as it is for processes engaging the public.

Fifth, the process should focus on **effectiveness** of the framework not efficiency alone. Here, we mean that attempting to keep costs low should be viewed within the context of what needs to be done. Often, for example, public engagement is viewed as an "added cost" for public land planners, and meetings are often perceived as simply a means of collecting data about public preferences.

Finally, these frameworks will function most effectively when we think at the **systems level**. Systems thinking involves considering relationships across time, space, and function. For example, one might consider how employment of a framework might help create an understanding of how actions on a particular site might impact conditions and use levels at other places. Thus, managers must be willing to consider regional consequences or effects occurring at longer time scales (McCool and Cole 2001).

Framework Summary

A growing number of recreation issues confronting public land managers occur within a context of complexity, change and uncertainty, and declining organizational capacity. These conditions accelerate the need for frameworks to assist mangers in working through these challenges. Relatively few effective, field-tested frameworks exist for this array of issues, suggesting that (1) managers may have difficulty finding a suitable framework and (2) there is need to develop frameworks for future issues and situations.

For now, public land recreation planners have choices to make about which framework is most useful for which situation or issue. In making this decision, they need to consider organizational capacity and commitment to complete the framework, hold reasonable expectations about how the framework will help them, and be informed about the capabilities, strengths, and weaknesses of the frameworks available. Of these three factors, the last two are the subject of chapter 4.

Chapter 4: A Primer on Recreation Planning Frameworks

In this section, we provide a primer on the assortment of recreation planning frameworks that managers may choose to address the variety of issues confronting them in contemporary public land management situations. By primer, we mean an introduction to the framework, which includes an understanding of why and how a particular framework evolved, what were the contexts under which it developed, how it has been applied, and how it has worked out. Although a primer is not a detailed explanation, we do try to provide the reader with enough information about the framework to make a decision about its use in a particular situation. We also identify the key bibliographic resources that would be of assistance in implementing each of the frameworks.[1]

Each section below begins with a description of the historical development of the framework, including the context and a discussion of the primary issue it was designed to address and the requirements that are needed to implement it.

Following this descriptive section, we (1) provide an overview of managerial experience with the framework, (2) examine strengths and weaknesses, (3) discuss the barriers to implementation and (4) list some of the major lessons learned following implementation. These sections are provided for Recreation Opportunity Spectrum (ROS) and Limits of Acceptable Change (LAC) specifically. For Visitor Experience and Resource Protection (VERP) and Benefits-Based Management (BBM), our assessment is more limited, primarily because of the limited amount of managerial experience at this point.

Recreation Carrying Capacity
Developmental History

The notion that wildlands hold a specific, numerical-based capacity for recreation and tourism has existed for nearly three-quarters of a century beginning with Sumner's (1936) observation about impacts of recreation on trees in the Sierra Nevada. Recent interest began in the early 1960s as recreational use of wildlands

---

[1] We have generally excluded the grey literature in this assessment, for accessibility of literature is an important characteristic in considering choices.

began to grow dramatically. As debate on designation of some of them as wilderness occurred, increased interest developed over the biophysical impacts of recreation. Several articles during the 1960s in the popular newspaper journal *Christian Science Monitor* reflected these concerns and argued that national parks were being "loved to death."

During this period, the USDA Forest Service initiated several research projects (initially titled as cooperative recreation research units and located at university campuses) to identify carrying capacities for recreation. These research units, and inter-nal Forest Service research, were a result of a problem analysis in the late 1950s that suggested that research focus on establishing recreational carrying capacities (Dana 1957). One of the first publications from this research, "*The Recreational Capacity of the Quetico-Superior Area*" (Lucas 1964) reflected these initial notions that landscapes contain a fixed upper limit to the number of visitors that can be accommodated. However, Lucas found that motorboaters and canoeists held sub-stantially different attitudes toward each other, thus complicating the calculation of a carrying capacity based on visitor attitudes.

At this time, research and management implicitly assumed that use levels and impacts were related linearly. However, the existence of an innate or intrinsic carrying capacity would suggest a J-shaped curvilinear relationship between use and impact. Such a relationship, if documented, would indicate that impacts rise slowly in response to recreational use and then reach a threshold beyond which conditions deteriorate rapidly. The threshold region of this curve would then represent the carrying capacity for tourism and recreation. The early research on the question (Lucas 1964, Wagar 1964) suggested that there appeared to be both biophysical and social carrying capacities, observations that carry on in today's research and management. Wagar even argued that social capacities would differ depending upon the motivations tourists sought during a visit to wildlands, an argument similar to Carey's (1993) implication that Maslow's need hierarchy would suggest a variety of human carrying capacities depending on what needs should be addressed. Wagar (1964) presented a series of graphs that served to hypothesize the relationship between recreation use level and ability to achieve certain desired outcomes of the recreation experience, such as challenge, solitude, and companionship. The curves were frequently differently shaped, suggesting, in schematic form, potentially *different* capacities for a particular site or location, based not on biophysical impacts but on sociopsychological factors.

Following these initial efforts, a variety of researchers in the United States engaged in additional work in the late 1960s and 1970s that culminated in a series of observations about the carrying capacity issue (e.g., Frissell and Stankey 1972, Lime 1970, Lime and Stankey 1971, Stankey 1973). These and other scientists suggested that the *objective* for which an area was established was a critical element in determining carrying capacity, thus implying that for any area (as implied by Wagar's research), there were multiple carrying capacities: "no single capacity can be assigned to an entire area" (Lime 1970: 9). The fundamental implication of this suggestion was that a carrying capacity is more a function of social values than an innate characteristic of the landscape, the finding that Lucas developed out of his initial research in the early 1960s. These scientists also indicated that recreational use induces both quantitative and qualitative changes in both the biophysical and social character of the environment, leading to the question of how much and what type of change would be *acceptable*–a question that could be best addressed through understanding the objectives established for the area, the various causes of impacts, and public preferences. And, they suggested that social capacity appeared to be a function of visitor motivations and expectations. Finally, the realization that carrying capacity is a function of social values, and that any amount of recreational use leads to some level of impact (even if it cannot be measured with the extant technology) means that degradation cannot be prevented if recreational use is allowed. Put another way, degradation is an inevitable result of recreational use.

Carrying capacity is more a function of social values than an innate characteristic of the landscape.

Much of this research was initially conducted in recently designated wilderness, managed under provision of the Wilderness Act of 1964, and requiring that each wilderness provide "…outstanding opportunities for solitude …" Thus, the interest in a social carrying capacity, linked to the ability of visitors to achieve solitude was a fundamental driver of these studies. The implication that any level of use leads to some level of impact (even if not measurable under current technology) was a significant advance in understanding, for it again reinforced the notion that management should be directed toward acceptable conditions. What was acceptable and to whom still remains an important question for scientists and managers.

The accelerating growth of use on Western U.S. whitewater rivers for rafting and kayaking stimulated a host of managerial attempts to establish carrying capacities beginning with Grand Canyon National Park in 1972. The park established a capacity of 96,500 user-days for boater floating the Colorado River through the park. The capacity was based on the use level that had occurred in 1971, not some studied evaluation of the relationship between use level and resulting impacts. This capacity was increased several years later to 169,500 following revisions in the park's river management plan, but the limit and how it is implemented remains contentious. A system to allocate this total among both commercial outfitters and private boating groups was implemented. A use limit is a specific policy that constrains the number of people allowed access to a recreation opportunity; it is not necessarily a capacity in the sense of prevention of degradation, although such use limits may reflect concerns about degradation of social and biophysical conditions.

"Carrying capacities" and the resulting policies limiting the amount of recreation use have been adopted by a variety of U.S. national park, wilderness, and protected areas since that time, although their form and implementing action (formal rule, management plan guidance) differs substantially. As knowledge and management experience grew, definitions of recreational and tourism carrying capacity also evolved from the initial two primary types (biophysical and social) to include a "facilities" capacity and others. Recreational carrying capacity came to be defined as the amount of recreational use allowable by an area's management objectives.

Throughout the 1970s and 1980s, as managers attempted to establish use limits for backcountry and whitewater river situations, such limits were increasingly controversial. Notably, the use limits (see McCool and Stankey 1991 for a discussion) were portrayed as a "carrying capacity" and for the most part mimicked existing use levels. Not one case was proposed where the capacity was less than the existing level at which use was occurring, despite concerns that such areas were overcrowded. Each policy was established with a unique, and often controversial, methodology. In Glacier National Park, for example, backcountry camping capacity was based on one ranger's estimate of "what was good" for the backcountry. Along the Middle Fork of the Salmon River, the number of groups that could physically enter the river at the launching point (with the facilities that were available at the time) was a key variable in establishing a recreational carrying capacity for the river. The Grand Canyon National Park used use levels and characteristics occurring in the previous year, ignoring the dynamic character of visitor use patterns.

As managers gained experience with use limit policies (portrayed as carrying capacities) the idea of capacity was refined. For some managers, it became the amount of **degradation permitted** in an area's use management objectives rather than the number of visitors permitted. Eventually, carrying capacity was defined as the "acceptable" amount of human-induced **change** permitted in the management

Table 2—A representative contemporary definition of recreation carrying capacity

Carrying capacity	Definitions
Recreation	The level of use beyond which the recreation resource or recreation experience deteriorates
Biophysical	The maximum number of people that can use a given area for a specified period without reducing that area's ability to sustain use
Social	The maximum number of people that can use a given area for a specified period without reducing the level of satisfaction received by any of those persons on the area
Managerial carrying capacity	The maximum number of people that can be accommodated on a given area for a specified period and (a) not degrade the environment beyond a given level of acceptability, and (b) provide a given level of satisfaction for a given percentage of the users, as set by the recreation manager's objectives for the area

Note the emphasis on number of users and the notion of deterioration of conditions.
Source: British Columbia Ministry of Forests 1991.

goals established for an area. Note that this latter definition is not related to numbers of visitors at all, but rather the levels of impact judged acceptable. Who should make these decisions of acceptability? This question has plagued managers ever since. Table 2 provides a contemporary example of how recreation carrying capacity is defined.

More recently other scientists have attempted to develop tourism capacities for a variety of destinations at different scales, including Nepal, the Maldives, and a region of Cyprus (Brown et al. 1997, Saveriades 2000). Usually, these attempts were not informed by research and other scholarly activity critical of the carrying capacity notion. This resurgent interest in carrying capacity as a framework for management has also occurred for public lands and resources in the United States. For example, a 2003 report (Lake Ripley Management District 2003) defined recreation carrying capacity on a lake as "that threshold at which the number, type, and manner of operating watercraft will adversely impact boater safety, user satisfaction, and ecologic sustainability of the lake." What number, type and manner of watercraft operations **adversely** impacts conditions was not established.

A recent report by a Department of the Interior task force and related published articles (e.g., Haas 2004) have stimulated new interest in recreation carrying capacity and have strongly argued that establishing capacities (visitor capacities) can resolve many of the complex issues confronting public land managers. Some of this work has reverted to earlier definitions of recreational carrying capacity, for example, Haas (2002) defined visitor capacity as "the prescribed number of visitors at one time that will be accommodated." Although this recent definition does not refer to degradation of resources or values, the lack of reference to such determinations further confuses the notion of capacity.

Thus, recreation carrying capacity continues to play a key role as a management and research paradigm in administration of public lands in the United States and elsewhere. The changing and vague definitions and lack of scientific support coupled with popular interest has plagued the application of the concept, an issue we will return to later.

The vast array of definitions and discussions about carrying capacity has generally been absent key descriptions of processes and frameworks to identify it in specific locales. No one has developed a generic process, framework, or set of steps that could be used in developing a carrying capacity. There has often been confusion (see lessons learned below) between carrying capacity as a concept, policies that limit use, and alternative approaches to managing impacts (such as limits of acceptable change). Therefore, this section does not provide a specific description of a specific recreation carrying capacity framework.

> **The vast array of definitions and discussions about carrying capacity has generally been absent key descriptions of processes and frameworks to identify it in specific locales.**

Key Concepts and Premises

Frissell and Stankey (1972) suggested that carrying capacity is the "amount of change in an area" that is permitted by an area's management objectives (which could be defined as statements of desired conditions). This argument means determining how much change is acceptable is a social judgment, informed by science, but made in the milieu of political and ethical discourse (Krumpe and McCool 1997). Science does play a critical role in this process. It provides the knowledge that managers and citizens use in determining how much change is acceptable. It can inform planning processes about the linkages and relationships that exist in an area and with its context. It helps all of us understand the consequences of choosing different alternatives. Frissell and Stankey typified change as coming in two forms: natural and human-induced. Carrying capacity is focused on human-induced changes, but these changes can be hidden by natural variations caused by climate, soil, extreme events (fires, floods, etc.). Management objectives are statements of desired conditions, which may be different from current conditions.

The assertion that there is an intrinsic capacity or limit to the number of users in a recreation area is a specific ramification of a Malthusian view of the world: that is, there is a fixed and limited supply of resources, that institutions have little impact on allocation (and thus efficiency and equity issues), and that generation and dissemination of knowledge have small roles in changing the supply available.

Applied biologists, such as wildlife and range managers, have articulated this view with the notion that habitats and pastures have fixed abilities to provide forage (and/or cover) for animals; this is commonly referred to as "carrying capacity." Intrinsic to this notion is the assumption that a carrying capacity is inherent and cannot be modified, an assumption that is of course violated with every new wild-life or range plan. The question with which these fields were confronted dealt with the physical capacity of a particular pasture, range or wildland area to maintain over time the amount and quality of forage to sustain a specific number of stock, whether domestic or wild. In those fields, the issue initially was relatively straight-forward then became more complicated as scientists and managers began to under-stand how particular developments and practices (e.g., fences, salt, water tanks, pasture rotation, grass seeding, rest-rotation grazing systems) could enlarge the capacity of a particular area. It was quickly recognized that different sized animals (e.g., deer, cattle) had different quantitative and qualitative forage or browse re-quirements, thus indicating that range carrying capacity was a function of land-owner objectives as well as characteristics of the environment.

Another major premise underlying the notion of carrying capacity is that the system of concern is stable and unchanging. Of course, ecologists and sociologists now recognize that both biological and social systems are dynamic, subject to disturbance processes, complex (e.g., nonlinearly dynamic) and filled with uncer-tainty. If a system is stable and unchanging, then a carrying capacity might be established as a fixed number. However, when the system is in a state of flux, such a numerical description is not only scientifically invalid, but not useful as well.

Assessment of Experience With Recreation Carrying Capacity

Beginning in the late 1970s, as increasing number of users and scientists began questioning the underlying assumptions of recreation carrying capacity (e.g., Stankey and McCool 1984, Wagar 1974, Washburne 1981). There was a growing realization that carrying capacity itself was a simplistic view of the complex nature of recreational engagements, recreational settings, and recreational policy. The

There was a growing realization that carrying capacity itself was a simplistic view of the complex nature of recreational engagements, recreational settings, and recreational policy.

search for a recreational carrying capacity (often informally portrayed as a "magic" number) became constrained because the objectives of many protected areas are so broad or vague (e.g., "protect the resource") that they neither provide the specificity needed to provide clear direction for management nor establish numerical carrying capacities. These vague objectives can be interpreted in many different ways, leading again to many different capacities. In addition, the process of articulating objectives and selecting among them is a uniquely human and political process; the Earth itself does not speak in this process, and neither does science (although scientists may speak wearing the hats of concerned citizens).

If capacity is so dependent on objectives and if there are many potential objectives leading to many capacities for the same area, then what role could science play in informing this process? The observation that carrying capacity–and the amount of change acceptable–is dependent on objectives was a key advance in the development of the field of recreation and tourism management. It forced managers and scientists to be more explicit and specific about what objectives were in play in a specific area. It also led to the realization that development and choice of objectives is a social, not a physical or biological, process. Some authors (e.g., Shelby and Heberlein 1986) have used the terminology "carrying capacity," but essentially their approach does not necessarily lead to establishing a numerical carrying capacity.

Unfortunately, the importance of specific, explicit, and output-oriented objectives in establishing a carrying capacity, or directing management for that matter, has not translated into actual practice. Objectives identified in contemporary recreation plans are still plagued by vagueness and ambiguity. For example, the 1995 Grand Canyon National Park General Management Plan established this objective for recreation use of the Colorado River: "Provide a variety of primitive recreational activities consistent with Wilderness and National Park Service (NPS) policies on accessibility." This objective does not provide the level of specificity needed to establish a carrying capacity, for there are many interpretations of what constitutes a primitive recreational activity.

The experience of recreation carrying capacity in resolving the complex and often contentious issues associated with recreation and tourism development on public lands is uniformly a failure. Not only have intrinsic numerical carrying capacities failed to be identified, but policies limiting use (often portrayed as carrying capacities) often have been unsuccessful in resolving the issue instigating the search for a capacity. We come to this conclusion for three reasons: (1) carrying capacity is a misframing of the use-impact problem, (2) the theoretical foundation for recreation carrying capacity is invalid, and (3) practical implementation of carrying capacity in wildland settings is difficult.

The use-impact problem (either in biophysical or social domains) has been inappropriately framed as a question, "How many is too many?" Although the concerns underlying this question reflect deep anxieties about the sustainability of resources, they are better framed as, "What are the acceptable conditions?" for a particular area. Framing the question in this manner allows managers to separate means from ends, and positions a use limit policy as only one of a number of possible actions. If impact is an inevitable consequence of use, then the question must shift to what is acceptable. Acceptability, of course, is a value judgment, and thus arriving at this would require the explication of various value systems and the integration of the consequences of differing definitions of acceptability.

Second, the notion of carrying capacity is based upon questionable neo-Malthusian assumptions that populations grow exponentially, but are eventually limited so growth occurs in a logistic pattern. Population growth then is eventually limited by a variety of environmental factors (Seidl and Tisdell 1999). However, changes occurring in these environmental factors, biotic or abiotic, are caused by the population itself or by other factors. Natural variation in the environment indicates that a logistic determination of a single carrying capacity is all but impossible. Seidl and Tisdell (1999: 401) concluded: "...the concept of carrying capacity can only be calculated for deterministic and slightly variable systems, and only for cases where behaviour and ecological relationships of the species change slowly on the human time scale." Thus, even in the case of the animal populations that carrying capacity was originally designed to address, the highly varying character of the environment, the nonlinearly dynamic nature of many cause-effect relationships and lack of knowledge introduce considerable uncertainty into calculation of carrying capacities.

The insistence that a numerical recreation or tourism carrying capacity exists has been strongly refuted, not only recently (McCool and Lime 2001) but in a series of journal articles and book chapters (e.g., Stankey and McCool 1991, Wagar 1974, Washburne 1982). As yet, no proponent of the use of carrying capacity as an approach to manage recreation has responded substantively to these criticisms.

Such carrying capacities are also based on a number of cultural and scientific assumptions, the validity of which has been subject to a variety of recent criticisms

(Borrie et al. 1998, Seidl and Tisdell 1999). For example, a key assumption has been that land managers have the capability and means to control or influence both the occurrence of physical and social impacts and their mitigation. This assumption has been reinforced as scientific knowledge about the relationships between use and impacts has developed, giving managers confidence and the expectation that they can control complex biophysical and social processes. Neither the effectiveness nor efficiency of any particular use limit policy has been reported in the literature (McCool 2001), however, and only scant attention has been given to their equity effects (e.g., Stankey and Baden 1977).

These criticisms lead to two fundamental conclusions: (1) there is no such thing as an intrinsic or innate carrying capacity; and (2) an area may have multiple capacities, depending upon what objective is articulated for the area. Thus, an individual protected area–say a marine park–may have a very low capacity if it is designed to provide opportunities for solitude in a pristine setting; or a higher capacity, if the objective is to provide opportunities that are more social in character and where there are fewer constraints on the impacts caused by the recreating public. Obviously, there could be multiple (and even an infinite number of) capacities for objectives between these extremes. If one area can have multiple capacities, does the concept of capacity have any managerial utility? The search for a capacity, then, is highly dependent on selection of a specific objective (Lime 1970).

Although these foundational assumptions and a variety of others are open to question and have been seriously challenged in a broad array of venues (McCool and Lime 2001, Roe 1997, Seidl and Tisdell 1999, Wagar 1974), carrying capacity itself has often been used to justify limitations on access to public lands. Although the conceptualization of carrying capacity as some fixed, intrinsic capability of a landscape has evolved—primarily away from a focus on numbers to more emphasis on acceptable conditions, there remain significant issues in its formulation, conceptual validity, and managerial utility.

> **If one area can have multiple capacities, does the concept of capacity have any managerial utility?**

Lessons Learned

1. Carrying capacity requires specific objectives, but agencies are often reluctant to develop those objectives.

Vaguely written objectives, such as "protect the resource" or "provide a diversity of high-quality recreational opportunities" are subject to wide interpretation and debate. These objectives are not specific enough to use in establishing a carrying capacity. Carrying capacity, like other managerially useful concepts, requires not only informed judgment, but agreement on objectives. Although most people could probably agree that "protecting the resource" is an acceptable objective, the statement is so broad that it may hide fundamental disagreements among those who think they agree. The objectives of most recreation management plans are written so vaguely, a specific carrying capacity cannot be established from them.

We've used the term "reluctant" to describe agency development of objectives, primarily because the literature has identified characteristics of useful recreation objectives for more than two decades (Schomaker 1984, e.g., presents a list of five criteria). Agencies have generally chosen implicitly or explicitly not to develop objectives that meet these criteria.

2. Because carrying capacity is a function of objectives, there are many carrying capacities for a site; if there are many, the concept loses its utility.

Identifying and agreeing on objectives for an area is a uniquely human activity requiring judgment, deliberation, and agreement. Science plays an important role in helping those involved assess the consequences of alternative objectives. Because an area may have more than one potential objective, it follows that the area may have more than one possible carrying capacity for recreation. Therefore, there is no "innate" carrying capacity, and there is no universally defined point beyond which degradation occurs. Because there can be many carrying capacities for one area (based on the array of potential objectives) the concept thus has little practical utility.

3. For most recreation management situations, impact issues are more a function of visitor behavior or development actions than numbers.

A variety of research, both biological (e.g., Leung and Marion 2000) and social, shows that visitor behavior is a principal cause of impacts. Carrying capacity is focused on **numbers** of visitors, and thus is unlikely to resolve the impact issues that are related to behavior. The confusion is often reinforced by simplistic orientations toward capacity as a function of perceived "crowding," where respondents in a study are asked to identify how "crowded" a particular area is. Then, scientists, using these perceptions of crowding make some judgments about what point on the scale such judgments represent a "capacity." In many cases, an average score is used, ignoring the early precept that in recreation "there is no such thing as an average camper." For example, Rischbieter (2004) in reporting on the social carrying capacity of a reservoir in California indicated that because the average score on a perceived crowding scale was 3.3 on a scale of 1 to 9, that crowding, and thus social capacity was not an issue. The fact that it might have been an issue for some subgroups having expectations of solitude was neither studied nor reported.

4. There is often confusion in the literature about the nomenclature: carrying capacity, use limit policies, and processes such as limits of acceptable change.

Often, management plans state that a "carrying capacity" has been or should be established for an area. But actually, what such plans have done is to limit use—by day, week, or season, for example. Such use limits are one of many approaches to managing recreation use and impact issues. Other techniques, such as information, education, site hardening, and so on are also available. Use-limit policies are designed to achieve certain objectives, which reflect the desired social and biophysical conditions identified for an area. They are not an end in themselves.

In addition, there is often confusion between carrying capacity and frameworks for identifying appropriate conditions. For example, limits of acceptable change (see below) is often identified as an approach for **identifying** carrying capacity. Quite to the contrary, processes such as limits of acceptable change were developed as **alternatives** to carrying capacity not a method to establish it. Use of the term "carrying capacity" in such different ways makes communication, and thus understanding, very difficult.

5. The conditions needed to establish a carrying capacity are often not present on a recreation site.

For a carrying capacity to be established for an area, a number of practical and conceptual conditions must be present (McCool 1989, Shelby and Heberlein 1986). These conditions include the following:

- There is agreement on the type of recreation opportunity to be provided.
- The recreation opportunity is density dependent.
- The management agency controls access to the area.
- There is a clear and specific relationship between use level and biophysical or social conditions.
- Visitation level is more important than behavior in determining impacts.
- There is agreement on the objective of a rationing system to implement the capacity or use limit.
- The agency has the resources to administer the capacity.

- There is agreement on the acceptable level of impact.
- There is agreement that the capacity is the maximum tolerable use level or the optimal use level.

Unfortunately, for most situations, only a few, at most, of the above conditions are present, making implementation of a carrying capacity arbitrary at best.

Thus, carrying capacity is identified as only a pseudo-framework: there is little scientific evidence for the existence of a numerical capacity; no process for developing a numerical estimate based on scientific relationships between causes and effects has ever been established; the conditions needed to establish and implement it in the field are rarely present; and although some scientists prefer to use the term as an umbrella for use management problems, this is a very poor communication device.

6. Because carrying capacity is a technical approach to fundamentally value-laden problems, there is little room for public engagement.

Carrying capacity is a theory of the relationship between use level and impact; as such it relies more on science than public and experiential knowledge. As a result, the process of establishing a carrying capacity leaves little substantive room for open and deliberative processes that emphasize learning. In addition, because carrying capacity is based more on numbers of individuals, there are substantial questions regarding its effectiveness in controlling or limiting impacts, as such impacts are largely a function of other variables.

Recreation Opportunity Spectrum
Developmental History

The Recreation Opportunity Spectrum (ROS) is the best known of the frameworks presented here. ROS, however, is both a framework and a concept, which in turn is constructed upon other concepts and premises as described below. In this section, we review the history of the development of ROS in terms of it being both a concept and a framework.

Although the concept of a spectrum of recreation opportunities has a long history in the field of outdoor recreation management (going back to papers by J. Alan Wagar—*Campgrounds for Many Tastes* and *Quality in Outdoor Recreation*, published in 1963 and 1966, respectively—(Wagar 1963, 1966) and E.L. Shafer— *The Average Camper Who Doesn't Exist* (Shafer 1969),[2] it was not until the passage of the National Forest Management Act (NFMA) of 1976 that the idea took hold and was eventually implemented. These early papers discussed the notion that not all people visiting forested landscapes preferred similar settings, were looking for comparable experiential outcomes, or desired equivalent facilities. These papers put forth the proposition that the way to achieve quality recreational experiences would be to provide a variety of facilities, settings, and physical environments—an argument at the foundation of several later papers on this concept (see especially Clark 1982, Clark and Stankey 1979).

However, the concept of a spectrum lay relatively dormant for many years. But in the 1970s, rapid growth in recreational use, dramatic increases in harvested timber volumes, and a rising environmental consciousness led to an enormous and continuing debate not only about the purposes of publicly administered lands but also about how they should be managed. Controversies on the Bitterroot (Montana) and the Monogahela (Pennsylvania) National Forests in the early 1970s (concerning silvicultural techniques and visual quality) resulted in passage of the NFMA. Similar legislation, but with a somewhat different social and political foundation, occurred with respect to lands administered by the USDI Bureau of Land Management ([BLM] the Federal Land Policy and Management Act [FLPMA]). A fundamental premise of NFMA was that all uses and values of public lands must be considered in decisions and plans. In particular, NFMA required that forest plans provide for outdoor recreation opportunities and that timber harvesting decisions consider the effects on recreation.[3]

But how could recreational values, for example, be considered in management? Uses such as recreation were to be integrated with other values through the NFMA forest planning process and development of environmental statements. No framework existed that could state these values in ways that directly related to the social, regulatory, and biophysical condition of national forests, nor was a framework available that could describe the attributes of a recreational setting in the language of forest management. Extant efforts concerning recreation were also limited in

[2] We recognize that even as early as 1933, some, including Bob Marshall, recognized the notion, in a formal sense of a diversity of recreation opportunities.

[3] We recognize that the Multiple Use-Sustained Yield Act of 1960 identified outdoor recreation as one of the five uses of national forests; it wasn't until NFMA, however, that the Forest Service was specifically required to consider it and consequences to it in management plans.

their ability to describe the notion of diversity in recreation that had been expressed in the early literature. And there was no mechanism that could identify the impact to recreation, in terms of how opportunities would be affected, of alternative land uses and management actions proposed in the forest plans.

As these questions arose, scientists, working with managers, began to develop notions of how they could be addressed. The idea that settings—the place that managers manage—provide opportunities for experiences that are created by visitors and that a diversity of settings provides the route to quality recreation experiences formed the premises for their response. Settings are composed of a variety of attributes, such as user density, the amount and type of facilities, resource commodity production activities, and each of these attributes differs, thus facilitating some experiences and hindering others. By providing a diversity of settings, with varying attributes, over space, and with visitors aware of those opportunities, public land managers could ensure that quality experiences could be constructed by visitors. By focusing on settings—physical places with certain describable attributes—such a system would hold an inherent appeal to managers accustomed to dealing with management prescriptions that were place specific.

Settings are composed of a variety of attributes, and each of these attributes differs, thus facilitating some experiences and hindering others.

By formalizing these premises into a planning framework, managers and planners, in principle, would be able to address such questions as what would happen to the distribution of opportunities over a landscape when timber is harvested, what is the current spatial distribution of supply and what would it be under a new forest plan, and how could a particular setting be managed to reduce impacts on it? Such questions form the core of important allocation issues that are becoming not only increasingly complex but contentious as well as noted in chapter 2.

Beginning in 1978, the concepts of an **opportunity setting** and **spectrum of recreation opportunities** were formalized as a planning framework in a series of significant papers involving two groups of researchers working with public land managers: (1) Roger Clark and George Stankey (Clark and Stankey 1979) and (2) Perry Brown and Bev Driver (Brown et al. 1978, Driver and Brown 1978, Driver et al. 1987). The series of papers that evolved described the rationale, criteria, and linkages that could be made to other resource uses. The goal of these papers was to articulate the concept of an opportunity spectrum and to translate it into a planning framework; today they serve to archive the fundamental rationale behind the ROS concept and planning framework. The ROS framework as a planning framework was oriented toward integrating recreation into the NFMA required forest management plans. Both the BLM and the Forest Service eventually developed procedures and user guides to do this (e.g., USDA FS 1982).

The ROS, following its initial applications and tests, has been widely adopted around the world by various agencies in a wide variety of settings. Versions of it have been developed for tourism (Butler and Waldbrook 1991, Dawson 2001), water (Haas et al. 2004), hiking (Robson and Eagles 2002), mountain biking (Cessford 1995), urban settings, private lands (More et al. 2003), and even interpretation (Wearing and Archer 2003). The ROS is at the heart of recommendations for managing and planning for tourism under the international Convention on Biological Diversity (2005). It is the most widely recognized recreation management concept around the world and probably the most single influential concept in recreation management and planning for public lands and protected areas.

Description of the Recreation Opportunity Spectrum

There are two descriptions of ROS: as a concept and as a planning process. We will discuss each in turn. The ROS is based on the notion that a recreational setting consists of three types of attributes, each varying along a continuum: (1) biophysical—the amount of human-induced and evident change in the natural environment; (2) social—the location, type, and amount of interaction, contact or encounters with other people during a recreational engagement; and (3) managerial—the amount, type, and intrusiveness of rules, regulations, and presence of agency staff. Attributes give a setting its value for recreation. Recreational experiences are then constructed by the visitor using the attributes as elements to amalgamate in varying combinations.

Each of these attributes may vary along a continuum. For example, biophysical attributes may vary from no change to highly modified environments. Social attributes may vary from many and frequent encounters to few and rare. Figure 1 shows schematically the variance of each of the three attribute types. Roughly speaking, the continua are highly correlated, e.g., highly developed settings are also often typified by large numbers of encounters and many rules and regulations. There are exceptions (described as inconsistencies) of course, as noted below. Figure 2 illustrates the spectrum of recreation opportunities that results when the three attribute types are combined.

This concept then was translated into a planning framework by identifying specific factors to consider for each attribute, mapping them, and then providing guidelines for classifying specific sites into one of several categories developed along the continuum. The classification system would function to reduce the

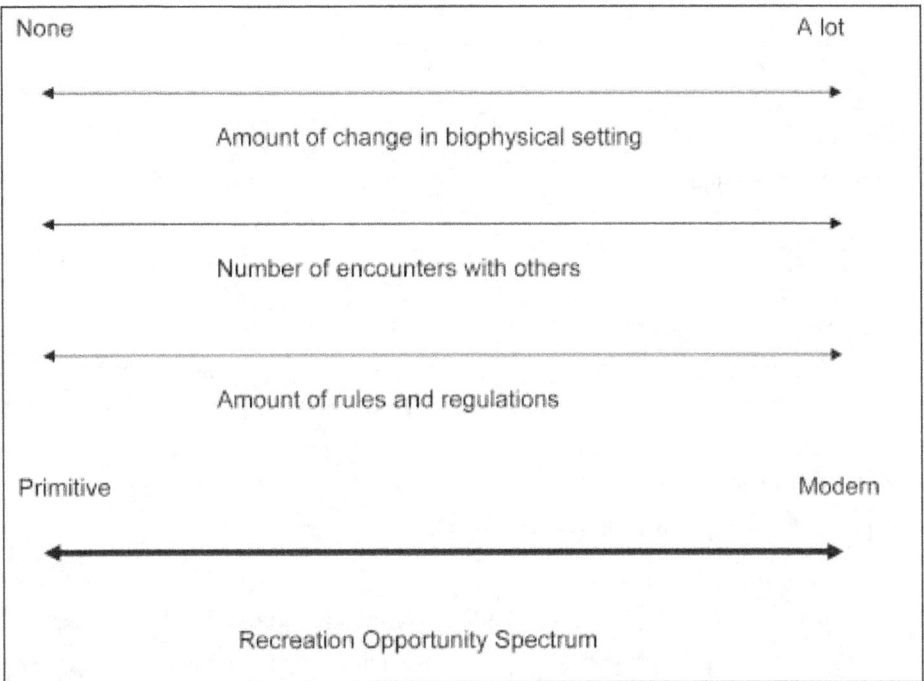

None   A lot

Amount of change in biophysical setting

Number of encounters with others

Amount of rules and regulations

Primitive   Modern

Recreation Opportunity Spectrum

Figure 1—The Recreation Opportunity Spectrum is described by continua concerning the biophysical, social, and managerial attributes. The combination of the three gives rise to a continuum of settings.

Primitive	Semi-Primitive non-Motorized	Semi-Primitive Motorized	Roaded Natural	Rural	Modern

Figure 2—The spectrum resulting from the inventory and mapping processes is divided into several classes to ease interpretation and management. Here six classes fairly typical of Forest Service ROS planning are depicted.

number of "objects" or categories to a reasonable number for planning and management (as a line or continuum essentially represents an infinite number of points). The tabulation below lists the factors in developing ROS as a planning system that were originally suggested by both groups.

Clark and Stankey (1979)	Brown et al. (1978)
Access (difficulty, access system, means of conveyance)	Access
Other nonrecreational uses	Remoteness from sights and sounds of human activity
Onsite management (extent, apparentness, complexity, facilities)	Size of area
Social interaction	Amount of irreversible evidence of human activity
Acceptability of visitor impacts (degree of impact, prevalence)	Amount of apparent renewable resource modification
Acceptable level of regimentation	

Clark and Stankey (1979) proposed dividing the continuum into four classes; Driver and Brown (1978) suggested six classes. Managers in the Pacific Northwest Region (Region 6) of the Forest Service eventually identified 10. This variation in the number of suggested classes initially formed the basis of some confusion about ROS, but as experience with it as a concept that could be implemented differently in different places developed, such confusion was eliminated.

Although both Clark and Stankey and Driver et al. proposed specific attributes to measure, Clark and Stankey implicitly suggest that other attributes may be measured and used to define a spectrum as long as they are

- Observable and measurable
- Under managerial control
- Related to recreationists' preferences and affects their decisions about places to visit
- Characterized by a range of conditions

This set of criteria could conceivably be used to develop a spectrum of opportunities in very different ways than which Clark and Stankey applied it.

Using ROS as a planning framework involves several phases or components that vary a bit from one agency to another (see, e.g., USDA FS 1982, 1990). It is important to recognize that each component plays an essential part of ROS as a planning framework. The basic phases each address a different question (see table 3). They were initially described by Stankey et al. (1983) as follows:

Table 3—Principal questions addressed in each of the five major phases of the Recreation Opportunity Spectrum planning framework

Phase	Description	Principal question(s)
1	Description of current settings	What is happening at present?
2	Identification of alternatives	What can be happening?
3	Select preferred alternative	What should be happening?
4	Implement management	What will be happening?
5	Monitoring and evaluation	What happened?
		Why did it happen?
		What should be done?

Phase 1. Defining and describing the recreation setting. Land managers describe the setting by using specific setting attributes as the basis for inventory of the area. In many cases, these attributes include access (trail, road, paved, gravel), remoteness (distance from trails and roads), naturalness (visibility of resource management activities such as timber harvesting), presence of facilities and site management, amount and type of encounters with other people in the area, types and visibility of visitor impact, and visitor management activities such as rules, enforcement personnel, etc. (USDA FS 1990). These inventories are then used to map the existing set of ROS classes across the landscape. When areas are mapped by using these criteria (on Forest Service administered lands), they are placed into one of six possible classes: (1) primitive; (2) semiprimitive nonmotorized; (3) semiprimitive motorized; (4) roaded natural; (5) rural; and (6) urban, although exceptions occur (e.g., urban opportunities do not usually exist on Forest Service administered lands). We note here that the number of ROS classes may differ from application to application depending upon the objectives of the planning process.

Phase 2. Assessing alternative management regimes. This involves different ways of allocating lands to different ROS classes. This is distinct from phase 1, which identifies only the **existing** condition, not what **could** *be*. Each alternative reflects a somewhat different approach to provision of recreation on public lands, and thus leads to somewhat different allocations. The alternative management regimes are developed from differing philosophies of public land management. These allocations are displayed on maps and in tabular form.

Phase 3. Selecting the preferred alternative. This phase identifies what **should be**, given public land management objectives, other resource uses, regional supply and demand, public needs and values.

Phase 4. Implementing the preferred alternative. This phase establishes a management regime for what **will be**. Here, public land managers integrate the program development and integration activities across time and space to produce an optimal public land management program.

Phase 5. Monitoring and evaluating phase 4. Monitoring includes identifying what has happened—the consequences of implementation of the preferred alternative. It also evaluates the consequences, which addresses why these things are happening and what should be done, if anything.

Defining the setting is critical to the successful application of this process. Examples are shown in tables 4 and 5. The initial output of the ROS planning framework (phase 1) is an inventory of existing recreation opportunities. The product is a map, and potentially a tabular display of acreages, of existing setting opportunities by ROS class (see fig. 3 for an example).

There have been a number of Forest Service and agency variations to ROS inventory and mapping processes (and adaptations by a number of foreign governments, e.g., B.C. Ministry of Forests 1998), but the general approach remains the same. Although the Forest Service was the primary agency involved in developing ROS as a planning system, other federal and state agencies have applied ROS to lands they administer.

Key Concepts and Premises

The fundamental premise of ROS is that quality recreational experiences are best assured by providing a range or diversity of opportunities: by allowing visitors to make decisions about the settings they seek, there will be a closer match between the expectations and preferences visitors hold and the experiences they realize (Stankey 1999). Thus, underlying the ROS idea is the notion of a **spectrum** or diversity of opportunities that can be described as a continuum, roughly from developed to undeveloped. Such opportunities are described by the **setting.** A setting is defined as the combination of attributes of a real place that gives it recreational value. Settings are composed of the three types of attributes described earlier.

The ROS provides an important contribution to the literature of recreation management with the idea that there are different "levels" of demand. The **recreation demand hierarchy** (Driver and Brown 1978) was developed to describe these levels and their linkages. The ROS as a planning system is best understood within the context of this concept (fig. 4).

> The fundamental premise of ROS is that quality recreational experiences are best assured by providing a range or diversity of opportunities.

Table 4—Typical example of Recreation Opportunity Spectrum (ROS) class descriptions[a]

ROS class	Physical setting	Social setting	Managerial setting
Primitive	Area is characterized by essentially unmodified natural environment of fairly large size.	Concentration of users is very low and evidence of other users is minimal.	Only facilities essential for resource protection are used. No facilities for comfort or convenience of the user are provided. Spacing of groups is informal and dispersed to minimize contacts between groups. Motorized use within the area is not permitted.
Semi-primitive non-motorized	Area is characterized by a predominantly unmodified natural environment of moderate to large size.	Concentration of users is low, but often other area users are evident.	Facilities are provided for the protection of resource values and the safety of users. Onsite controls and restrictions may be present but are subtle. Spacing of groups may be formalized to disperse use and limit contacts between groups. Motorized use is not generally permitted.
Semi-primitive motorized	Same as semiprimitive nonmotorized	Same as semi primitive non motorized.	Same as semiprimitive nonmotorized; except that motorized use is permitted.
Roaded natural	Area is generally characterized by a generally natural environment. Resource modification and utilization practices are evident, but harmonize with the natural environment.	Concentration of users is low to moderate. Moderate evidence of the sights and sounds of humans.	Onsite controls and restrictions offer a sense of security. Rustic facilities are provided for user convenience as well as for safety and resource protection. Facilities are sometimes provided for group activity. Conventional motorized use is provided for in construction standards and design of facilities.
Rural	Area is characterized by a substantially modified natural environment. Resource modification and utilization practices are evident.	Concentration of users is often moderate to high. The sights and sound of humans are readily evident.	A considerable number of facilities are designed for use by large numbers of people. Facilities are often provided for specific activities. Developed sites, roads, and trails are designed for moderate to high use. Moderate densities are provided far away from developed sites. Facilities for intensive motorized use are available.

[a] These were developed for the Grand Staircase-Escalante National Monument in Utah, USA.
Source: USDI BLM 1998.

Table 5—Recreation Opportunity Spectrum (ROS) Midewin National Tallgrass Prairie

Setting indicators	Rural	Roaded natural	Semiprimitive
1. Experiences	a. High feeling of safety b. Many opportunities for facilitated discovery c. High social interaction d. Opportunity for solitude unlikely, low feeling of escape from sights and sounds of humans e. Low opportunity for challenge	a. Moderate-high feeling of safety b. Some opportunities for facilitated discovery c. Moderate-high social interaction d. Low opportunities for solitude, low feeling of escape from sights and sounds of humans e. Low opportunity for challenge	a. Moderate-high feeling of self-reliance b. Discovery is mainly dependent on self, but some opportunities for facilitated discovery may exist c. Low-moderate social interaction d. Medium-high opportunity for solitude, moderate feeling of escape from sights and sounds of humans e. Moderate opportunities for challenge
2. Physical setting (remoteness, size, and evidence of humans)	a. Highest level of development. New facilities may be somewhat abundant and visible, but in harmony b. Evidence of human influence on the landscape is abundant (buildings, roads, farmlands, plantings) c. Noticeably modified environment interspersed with a natural-appearing landscape d. Adjacent to and/or easy access to/from internal and external roads e. No minimum or maximum acreage	a. Moderate level of development. New facility development is minimal, subtle and in harmony with the natural environment b. Evidence of human influence on the landscape is present, primarily from external land uses c. Noticeably modified environment within primary natural-appearing landscape d. May be adjacent to external roads, adjacent to or including internal roads e. No minimum or maximum acreage	a. Lowest level of development. New facility development is very minimal, and in harmony with the natural environment b. Evidence of human influence on the landscape is primarily historic abandoned structures and does not detract from a natural experience c. Predominantly natural appearing environment d. At least ¾ mile from nearest internal auto road and internal transportation system; at least ½ mile from nearest external public road and railroad; 1/8 mile from bike, equestrian, and multiuse trails e. Minimum of 640 acres
3. Social encounters (user density, contact)	High probability of frequent social encounters, high probability of encountering large groups	Moderate probability of frequent social encounters, moderate probability of encountering large groups	Low-moderate probability of frequent social encounters, low probability of encountering large groups
4. Managerial control (restrictions)	Regimentation and controls are obvious and numerous and largely in harmony with the natural environment	Onsite regimentation and controls are noticeable and harmonize within the natural environment	Onsite regimentation present but subtle
5. Motorized administrative access	Yes	Yes	Yes, but limited
6. Automobile/road access	Yes	Yes	No
7. Shuttle or train	Yes	Yes	No

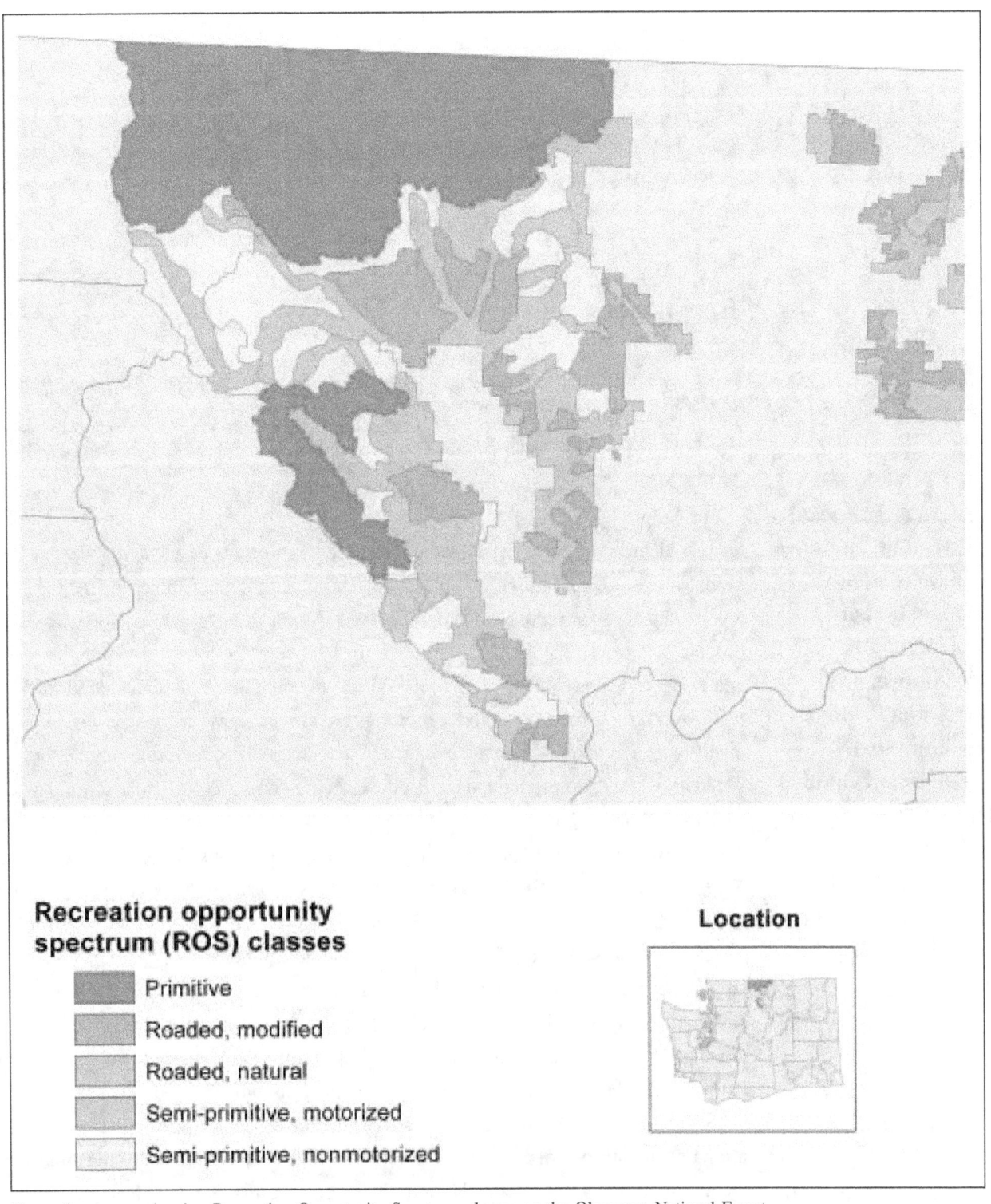

Recreation opportunity spectrum (ROS) classes

- Primitive
- Roaded, modified
- Roaded, natural
- Semi-primitive, motorized
- Semi-primitive, nonmotorized

Location

Figure 3—A map showing Recreation Opportunity Spectrum classes on the Okanogan National Forest.

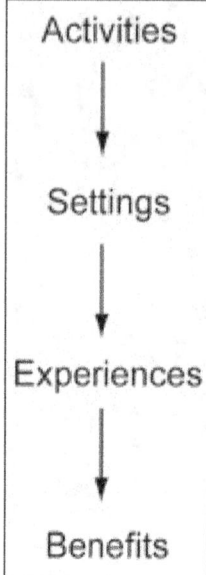

Figure 4—The recreation demand hierarchy (adapted from Driver and Brown (1978)). Demands for recreation occur at several levels, from specific activities (such as camping), through settings (e.g., roaded natural), through experiences (learning about nature) to benefits—improved conditions—such as family cohesiveness. Managers play a critical role in this hierarchy because the setting is essential for satisfactory experiences.

The demand hierarchy is so named because it represents demands for recreation at four levels, based on their complexity, visibility, and understandability.

The demand hierarchy is so named because it represents demands for recreation at four levels, based on their complexity, visibility, and understandability. At the top are demands for recreation activities—this is the form of recreation that we observe at various recreation settings, it is the behavior that individuals practice and display, such as water-skiing or fishing. At the next level are demands for the recreation settings described above. Settings are the places where the top-level demands occur, and an argument can be made that demands for activities are better stated as demands to participate in specific activities within a particular setting, such as backpacking in a remote, uncongested wilderness. At the third level, demands for recreation experiences are expressed. This means that people engage in certain recreation activities in particular settings in order to have satisfactory experiences. These experiences contain a number of dimensions. In essence, visitors select particular setting attributes, put them together in their head, and then construct an experience containing such dimensions as adventure, challenge, solitude, stress release, companionship, appreciating nature, freedom, escape and other dimensions of a recreational engagement. Helpful to understanding the notion of experience is the concept of **satisfaction**. Satisfaction may be defined in several ways, such as the realization of expectations, the difference between a person's normative definitions of a preferred experience and what is realized, or the attainment of that individual's defined quality experience. Unfortunately, the definitions of satisfaction have been controversial in the recreation research literature, and various studies of this concept have not proved to be particularly helpful to managers.

At the fourth level of the demand hierarchy is the notion of **benefit**. Benefits are the "improved" conditions experienced by individuals, small groups, and society at large as a result of satisfactory recreational engagements. If individuals receive a satisfactory recreational experience, benefits will result. These benefits may involve reduced family divisiveness, greater worker productivity, or reduced crime.

However, not all recreational experiences are satisfying. Visitors interact with settings and their individual attributes, and those settings may be significantly different from their expectations—more or less developed, more or less congested, for example—and as a result visitors decide not to return. Other visitors may feel those attributes lead to a satisfying experience, and thus **replace** the previous visitors. This process may also lead to **displacement** of less tolerant visitors by more tolerant ones. The process of displacement and replacement may be termed **visitor succession.** Visitor succession indicates that the visitors are sensitive, in many cases, to even relatively small changes in setting attributes, and that the preferences and expectations of current visitors may not be useful in determining what the setting should be like. Each successional wave of visitors leads to a situation where the next group of visitors are more tolerant of more developed (or more congested, more regulated) setting attributes than the previous group. Visitor succession may be one reason why, over time, a population of visitors at a specific setting may always seem satisfied.

Implementing Requirements

Of the frameworks identified in this paper, ROS is probably the easiest to implement. That said, it requires that agencies meet three requirements: (1) a commitment to implement the processes it involves; (2) a set of technical skills, including knowledge about recreation visitor motivations, experiences, and preferences, and geospatial analysis and data display; and (3) certain biophysical and social information. In this section, we present each of these three major requirements.

Agency commitment—

A commonly vocalized critique of ROS is that it is complicated and expensive to implement. We believe that it is no more complicated than frameworks managing any other natural resource on public lands, and in comparison to the complexities of the human behavior that it seeks to manage, it is actually relatively easy. These criticisms, however, reflect, we believe, organizational commitments to understand and provide for recreation opportunities. Many public land management agencies do not hire trained recreation specialists, and thus any recreation planning framework is likely to appear complicated to those not trained in using them. Thus, at a systemic level, agencies can commit themselves to higher quality recreation management by devoting the resources necessary to continuing education and training, and at the operational level by devoting the financial resources needed to conduct good ROS inventories.

Needed skills—

To conduct all phases of ROS and use it as a decision aid, agencies must hold a variety of knowledge areas, skills, and abilities. First, there must be basic knowledge about recreation use patterns, visitor expectations, preferences, and attitudes toward management. It may be sufficient that this knowledge is general, e.g., does not need to be developed for a specific area. This knowledge should also encompass the interaction of recreation with other uses—such as timber production—and values—such as aesthetics—in order to better understand the consequences of alternatives. The agency must have the technical capacity to implement the inventory and monitoring identified above, to analyze and display the data derived from the inventory, and to assess the consequences of alternatives. In this respect, ROS uses the same kind of sophisticated geographic information system technology as other uses and values of wildlands and can be easily brought into the system.

The ROS involves several phases: inventory, analysis, and presentation of data. In each of these phases, a variety of value judgments may be made. Agencies must hold the needed skills to think through these tasks, to the point of asking what the data will look like—which reflects the decision and information needs of managers—prior to collecting the data. Not working through data collection and display will often lead to a sense of frustration or considerable dilemmas in how to present and use the resulting data.

Information requirements—

The first phase of ROS involves conducting an inventory of settings, including managerial, biophysical, and social attributes. Agencies, such as the Forest Service, have developed specific manuals and guides to direct what variables should be measured, how they should be measured, and how they should be displayed (e.g., USDA FS 1990). To use ROS, then, an agency must have the ability to measure the specific variables called for in the manual (e.g., access type, remoteness). These variables are measured and then aggregated to specific, predefined opportunity categories. The agency must have the capability, generally in terms of a geographic information system, to conduct this analysis. Because a strength of ROS is its geospatial character, such variables must be measured across a landscape. Thus, the agency must have the capability to measure, analyze, and display these variables.

One of the uses of ROS, described in phase 2, is to develop alternatives and identify their consequences. A related use is to identify the consequences of other resource uses and values on a recreation opportunity. Thus, variables that measure and can be displayed geospatially would be required to conduct these assessments and tasks. Finally, it may be important to understand the distribution of ROS settings across landscape types. Thus, a description and geospatial distribution of landscape types is needed.

Assessment of Experience With Respect to the ROS

The ROS was initially implemented by both the USDA Forest Service and the BLM during the first round of their land management planning, as mandated by the respective planning acts (NFMA and FLPMA) during the mid 1980s. Both agencies developed manuals and instructions for implementation of the concept as a tool for integrating consideration of recreation values into land planning (e.g., USDA FS 1982). Later, ROS was integrated into the Forest Service visual and scenic management systems (e.g., The Built Environment Image Guide). Much of this implementation concerned **inventory** of existing recreation opportunities; some of it also involved **assessment** of impacts of specific proposed timber sales and associated road construction. Many of these assessments include identifying alternative sale and road regimes, leading to varying impacts to recreation opportunities.

Subsequent to this implementation, the concept of ROS rapidly disseminated outside these agencies and around the world. Currently, the concept of ROS, if not the specific implementation of it (as developed by the Forest Service and BLM) is used in a variety of national, state, provincial, and local recreation planning processes and is the most widely recognized concept in wildland recreation planning around the globe. Outside the United States, its most advanced application is in Australia and New Zealand, which resulted from a series of workshops in the early 1980s. In particular, the notion of diversity of opportunity, as reflected in zoning of settings, is a commonly used element of these planning processes. The widespread use of ROS suggests that it has filled an important need in natural resource planning.

The widespread use of ROS suggests that it has filled an important need in natural resource planning.

A major reason for the broad interest in ROS, we believe, is the collaborative nature of its initial development in the 1970s, involving both scientists (primarily Clark, Stankey, Brown, and Driver) and managers attempting to implement natural resource planning processes mandated by federal-level legislation. By collaborating, managers were able to communicate their needs, scientists were better able to understand these needs, and both were able to design a process that meets these needs. Importantly, because planning was being conducted at the forest or district level, the inventory and management costs were reasonable and the scale at which the ROS inventory and mapping was conducted seemed to be appropriate to the decisions being made. In addition, the process was not overly cumbersome, used tools (such as maps) with which managers were familiar, and was viewed as an integral component of planning and not as an "add-on." In short, ROS seemed to fit well into the culture of a natural resource organization that had little technical experience and expertise with respect to recreation planning.

Although initially the involvement of a variety of scientists led to some confusion among managers about such things as what to inventory and how many ROS classes there should be, the longer term result has been a process based on a strong theoretical or conceptual foundation meeting demands that decisions be based on the "best" available science. Only a few scientific articles have been written critical of ROS (e.g., Hamill 1984, Patterson et al. 1998). Even these criticisms are more operational than systemic in character. The widespread adoption of ROS also led to other scientists using the concept as a basis for identifying research needs and conducting specific studies.

As both managers and scientists gained experience with ROS, and as collaboration continued, the efficacy of implementation also increased. The arrival of computer-based geographic information systems at about the same time as the implementation of ROS also enhanced its use as a framework for examining interactions between recreation and other resource uses and values.

A major output of ROS was a map of a planning area displaying the spatial distribution of recreation opportunities. This was a distinct advance in resource management and enhanced the move away from reliance on tabular displays of data. Spatial relationships are critical to land management, be it wildlife, timber, or recreation. The ROS map, even if limited to what existed on the ground, carried many implications for managers of resource commodities, and some could have even viewed it as a threat because it now forced these other managers to display their resources and values in spatial form as well.

Although ROS has been successful as an inventory tool, it has been less successful in some other arenas of planning. Inventory of **what is** (descriptive), for example, can be easily confused with **what should be** (prescriptive): maps showing the **existing** distribution and classification of recreation settings were sometimes confounded with the idea that they represented an allocation in a plan of a set of **desired** conditions. This confusion is not a function of ROS, either as a planning framework or as a concept, but more of a realization of the implications of changing land uses. However, ROS did provide the opportunity for land planners to develop "what if" scenarios: What if a road was built up a drainage to support timber harvesting? How would that change the ROS classification? Would that change reflect larger scale and contextualizing land management objectives? Could the road and harvest design be changed themselves to minimize the impacts on recreation opportunities? Could the road and harvest design be changed to enhance a particular desired opportunity? What set of recreation opportunities should be offered where, and what would the impacts of those allocations be on other public land values? Unfortunately, this aspect of ROS capabilities is one of the most underutilized advantages of the system.

As ROS developed, individuals outside of agencies began to grasp the significance of ROS as a planning tool. Nongovernmental organizations (NGOs) in particular came to view it as a tool in their pursuit of high-quality land management. In one sense, ROS may have served as a surrogate for nonquantitative and noneconomic values of public lands. The NGOs pressured land management agencies to use ROS to better understand the consequences of alternative land management policies.

We noted earlier the recent extension of ROS into more specific recreation activities and settings. These attempts have met with mixed success. Textbooks and journal articles often cite ROS in the context of tourism (e.g., Boyd and Butler 1996, Dawson 2001, Newsome et al. 2002), and may even advocate use of ROS to assist in tourism, but few real world applications are reported in the literature. Many of these proposed applications have been developed by academics extending the basic premises to other settings, but not necessarily working collaboratively with end users.

Strengths and Weaknesses

The widespread adoption or ROS reflects its intrinsic appeal to managers and academics alike in providing a strong foundation to not only recreation and tourism decisions, but also in integrating recreation and tourism with other uses and values on public lands. The broad recognition of ROS as a concept and planning framework is one of its strengths in that there is relatively broad agreement as to its general meaning and use for recreation and tourism planning.

A second major strength of ROS is its ability to be relatively easy to use in making decisions about other resource uses and values and its use as a tool to quantitatively and spatially identify the consequences of these uses on recreation opportunities. This is strongly related to the inherently spatial quality of ROS, which is also a characteristic of other resource uses and values—such as timber production, wildlife habitat, watershed protection, and so on. This characteristic allows decisionmakers to better understand, spatially and quantitatively, the impacts of their decisions. Because of its intuitive appeal to managers, scientists, and publics, ROS can be effectively implemented, adopted in an open and deliberative process, and effectively protect a desired diversity of recreation opportunities.

ROS allows managers to think systematically about emerging issues and challenges.

Third, ROS allows managers to think systematically about emerging issues and challenges. For example, Clark and Stankey (1979) used ROS to work through the acceptability of noise in recreational settings. In their analysis, they considered the level of noise, its source and frequency, and how acceptable each might be in different ROS categories. And thus, they were able to develop guidelines that would be helpful to managers in making decisions about how to manage various sources of noise.

Fourth, as we have noted earlier, recreation management (as other areas of natural resource management) requires the use of judgments—either in selecting preferred alternatives, identifying key variables, or in determining objectives. The ROS provides managers with an explicit, scientifically-based process to make "state-of-the-art judgments" (Clark 1982) that are trackable and defendable. In making these judgments by using ROS to "work through" them, ROS forces managers to understand relationships and interactions, not only between settings and experiences, but between recreational and other resource values as well.

As with any planning framework, there are some weaknesses. First, there is often confusion between ROS as a concept and ROS as a framework that guides a set of planning processes. This confusion is illustrated by the (paraphrased) statement that occasionally is heard that ROS was developed for Western situations and not Eastern ones, and therefore does not apply. The ROS as a concept has significant empirical support in the scientific literature (e.g., Driver et al. 1987). Its implementation as a planning process, however, must be specific to a particular region or locale. Development of national-scale handbooks that establish specific criteria for locating a setting in one ROS class or another led to this confusion.

Implementation of ROS must occur within the context of regional supply-and-demand characteristics.

Development of ROS established a framework to structure thinking about recreation opportunities and how those opportunities would relate to other resource uses. That framework can be adapted, with creative thinking, to a number of situations—modern to primitive—and lead to appropriate classification of recreation opportunities. That classification can then be used to identify information needs, structure research, and understand consequences of alternative land uses. The framework—the ROS concept—is the foundation. The framework can be adapted, with creative thinking to a variety of situations, if planners can define the form of recreation in which they are interested, establish appropriate indicators of that recreation, and set standards for those indicators.

When ROS fails, it generally fails because of a rigid interpretation of standards or because data appropriate for the planning task have not been collected. For example, areas farther than 3 miles from a road are often classified as "primitive" in agency manuals. But areas do not have to be farther than 3 miles if there is intervening topography, vegetation, or other situational variables that provide the sense of isolation and remoteness that is important to primitive settings.

Second, ROS as a planning framework is not necessarily simple to use. It requires substantial data if implemented appropriately, considerable analysis and critical thinking applied to the inventory, and an ability to use it in a variety of multiple-use situations. Expectations that ROS involves application of prescriptive rules are inappropriate. It is a framework, supported by data and analysis, that helps managers work through often complex interactions between recreation and other resource uses and values. Managers should not expect answers from using ROS, but they should use it as a way of responding to increasing demands that public lands be used for a variety of purposes.

Barriers to Implementation

There are several significant barriers to implementation of ROS as a planning framework. Although these barriers may be important in any given situation, they are more operational than systemic in character. The most fundamental barrier to implementation of ROS is the lack of understanding of what it does and does not do within the context of multiple use-multiple-valued situations. As a result, ROS is often viewed as "lines on a map"; there is substantial confusion between what is and what should be, and the notion that ROS consists of six zones or categories. Implementation of ROS, as with any other natural resource management tool or framework requires in-service training and continuing education, organizational commitment to critical thinking and adaptive management, and a clear understanding of the planning question in any given situation.

A second barrier to implementation is the tendency to substitute judgments about conditions for actual inventory data. This situation is a result of a lack of willingness to invest in high-quality inventories for recreation. As a result, assessments of consequences of resource management alternatives to recreation opportunities are often marginally better than "guestimates." This barrier can be overcome, but only with a willingness to invest substantially in the inventory data during the early stages of planning. This is similarly a matter of organizational will.

A third barrier occurs when ROS is viewed as the "lines on a map" noted above without the needed understanding of the rationale behind how the lines were drawn. In this sense, ROS is often viewed mechanistically, as a well-defined and accepted procedure requiring little in the way of understanding. This is typical of bureaucracies, which are established to process and address routine problems, such as filling information requests, processing applications, and so on. Land management is anything but routine, however, and thus a bureaucracy would have difficulty in addressing unique problems. The only way around this particular barrier is for structural change to occur in agency approaches to land management—to move away from traditional rational comprehensive approaches to those that are more learning and adaptive management oriented.

Recreation Opportunity Spectrum Summary

The ROS planning framework has become an important tool for public land recreation managers. Undoubtedly, its intuitive appeal and ease of integration with other resource uses and values are responsible for its widespread adoption and modification. Its strong science foundation, and the collaborative nature of its initial development are probably also primary reasons why it has endured over a quarter century of natural resource planning. As a planning framework, ROS forces management to explicate fundamental assumptions, but in the process of moving through the framework, it allows reviewers to follow and understand results.

It has not only been useful for planning but it has spawned a great deal of research on recreation as well (e.g., Driver et al. 1987) and helped scientists formulate a variety of questions ultimately of use to managers. For example, what is the probability that certain setting attributes (e.g., use density) facilitate or hinder such dimensions of experiences as solitude? What is the linkage between settings and activity participation? Will satisfactory recreational experiences lead to longer term social benefits? How substitutable are settings?

Although ROS is popular and useful, it is also confronted by a number of challenges. Many of those (weaknesses and barriers to implementation) stem more from organizational factors than inherent weaknesses in the concept or how it has been implemented as a planning framework. Its continued applicability for the issues of the 21st century would benefit from a formal evaluation, similar in scope and content to what has been conducted for the Limits of Acceptable Change (LAC) framework (McCool and Cole 1997a, 1997b).

Lessons Learned

Here we provide a brief discussion of the important lessons learned in application of ROS.

1. Describing existing conditions is different from prescribing what should be—Early in the development and initial applications of the ROS, there was some concern that mapping the existing conditions would lead to those conditions being prescribed as a preferred alternative. As a result, there was some internal agency resistance to ROS. However, the intent of ROS was not to confuse description with prescription, but rather to provide decisionmakers a more comprehensive understanding of the consequences of decisions, primarily timber harvesting and road development, on the distribution and availability of recreation opportunities, and to do this in an explicit and scientifically based manner. Mapping what exists in terms of recreation settings is a far different exercise than prescribing what should be in, say, a forest plan.

2. Data aggregation is a potential problem—As a planning system, ROS requires that mapping be conducted in a cohesive and similar manner over a planning area. When two different planning agencies use different scales, criteria, or ROS classes, the quality of the resulting data over the entire planning area must be reduced to the "lowest common denominator." That is, if one jurisdiction only recognizes two categories, and another recognizes six, then the data for the entire area must be reduced to two categories to consistently display the mapped information. This reduces not only the quality of the data, but its usefulness for decisionmaking and wastes effort.

In this vein, however, agency policy may lead to a standard classification of ROS categories. Individual planning units within the agency may perceive a need for more categories, which must be balanced by agency-level needs and requirements. Designing ROS categories so they are "nested" within broader categories is a method to enable creativity at the local level and to retain the data reporting needs of higher organizational scales.

3. Dealing with "inconsistencies" remains an issue—As a ROS inventory proceeds, there will be instances where an "inconsistency" in the values of setting attributes occurs, for example, high-use densities in a remote, undeveloped setting, or a development in a remote, low-use setting (Sperry Chalet in Glacier National Park as an example). We note here that inconsistencies are likely to occur because ROS has **not** been used as a framework to understand and manage recreation. Clark and Stankey (1979) noted that the first step in dealing with an inconsistency is to better understand why it exists. In the case of Sperry Chalet, it is a "leftover" from a previous era when the park's backcountry was dotted with chalets to facilitate access by horse. It remains because it was made out of stone. Managers have treated inconsistencies in three ways: (1) "reduced" or moved the ROS class surrounding the inconsistency to a more developed class (e.g., primitive to primitive nonmotorized); (2) retained the class as if the inconsistency did not exist; and (3) "spot zoned" the inconsistency—the strategy employed in the NPS wilderness proposal for Glacier National Park. The circumstances for using each approach remain unclear. It is clear, however, that the context for inconsistencies is important to understand. Does a specific development at a site fit within the context? Is it appropriate, not only at the site level but the larger scale as well? Finally, we note that an apparent inconsistency, as in the case of Sperry Chalet, may actually lead to a different type of recreation opportunity.

4. Confusion between a landscape type and an ROS setting—As initially described by Clark and Stankey, recreation settings were independent of a particular landscape type, that is, a primitive setting could exist in undeveloped remote alpine settings as well as desert beach settings. They implicitly argued that the opportunity is similar in both situations. Recent research in Arctic settings (e.g., Lachapelle and McCool 2005b) suggests, however, that at least in some situations, the landscape may be so distinctively different that it produces a somewhat different opportunity. The ROS is based on an assumed linkage between settings and experiences; and although it has never been argued that this linkage is deterministic, there are situations where additional research is needed to better understand it.

5. Despite use of ROS, incremental changes in settings still occur—One fundamental reason for use of ROS in recreation management was to avoid incremental changes to the character of the setting (indeed, Clark and Stankey provided an outstanding example of such changes in the preface to their 1979 publication).

However, ROS has been viewed, at least implicitly, as more of a planning process (for large-scale decisions) than as a management or day-to-day decisionmaking tool. Thus, what appear to be small changes occurring incrementally (e.g., moving from pit toilets to flush ones, developing a boat launch ramp, paving a campground road) still occur without the kind of analysis that ROS was designed to assist. As a result, recreation opportunities are gradually moving to the more developed end of the spectrum.

6. Monitoring is essential if the ROS system is to be successful—If one thing characterizes the state of the art of public land recreation management it is uncertainty—not all consequences can be anticipated at the time of an allocation or management decision. Monitoring—the systematic and periodic measurement of key indicators—is essential to providing managers with the feedback needed to sustain the opportunities determined to be appropriate for a specific area. Monitoring provides at least two useful pieces of information: (1) it helps managers identify the impacts of any incremental or unanticipated actions on the supply of recreation opportunities, and (2) it forms a basis to strengthen understanding between opportunity setting attributes and experiences achieved by recreationists.

Monitoring is essential to providing managers with the feedback needed to sustain the opportunities determined to be appropriate for a specific area.

7. Implementation of ROS requires supporting continuing education and training—Like other technical planning systems, implementation requires carrying out the steps involved in ROS planning but also understanding the rationale and conceptual foundation to ROS. This capacity must be built not only with agency recreation planners but with managers implementing ROS on a day-to-day basis. Such training allows planners to better appreciate how ROS can be used and adapted in different situations.

8. Using ROS as a framework to estimate demand remains problematic—Recreation Opportunity Spectrum was developed primarily as a supply management tool. But if supply is defined by recreation settings, should recreation demand estimation use the same definitions? If we know how many acres in each ROS class are available, how would we know if this meets demand? How could demand for each ROS class be estimated? And what coefficients could be used, if any, to translate demand estimated in, say visitor-days, into acres? Such coefficients have been developed (e.g., USDA FS 1982, 1990) but only as examples and not as research-based findings. How valid is it to use coefficients? Perhaps more significantly, can we apply demand estimates spatially? Can we estimate which places are more attractive than others? Is the supply in the "right" place?

Variants and Derivatives

Recreation Opportunity Spectrum has been widely successful as an organizing framework, and as a result several variations to fit different situations have been developed. The most significant variation has been to apply ROS to destination tourism settings (Butler and Waldbrook 1991, Dawson 2001). Both attempts have received some recognition in the tourism literature, but there is little documentation of real world applications. Both reports identify a set of attributes (e.g., accessibility, infrastructure, degree of social interaction) and use those attributes to define a range or spectrum of settings. In this sense, the tourism opportunity spectrum is useful more at the regional scale and as a tool of mixed public-private organizations and ownerships that want to develop and manage a variety of destination attractions. However, in a capitalistic society, where each individual firm seeks to maximize profits and competes with others, there may be little immediate financial incentive to assign specific roles—parts of the spectrum—to specific businesses. Use of the ROS in this context would require substantial coordination and cooperation among a variety of businesses in a highly fragmented sector. Although these proposals have surfaced in the literature, they were developed largely outside of extended collaborative processes with destination marketing organizations willing to experiment. Thus, they may not become widely adopted as a planning tool.

Haas et al. (2004) similarly have applied ROS as a concept to water recreation opportunities. Although ROS as both a concept and planning tool contains this capability inherently, the Haas effort is designed to provide specific guidance to water settings, primarily those managed by the Bureau of Reclamation (see fig. 5 for an example of application). The Water Recreation Opportunity Spectrum (WROS) provides guidelines for applying the concept to water settings and using it to identify what recreation opportunities should be provided for and where in a water environment. In addition, the WROS handbook places emphasis on management once an allocation has been implemented. Because the WROS is relatively new, the viability of its specific application is unknown at this time.

Limits of Acceptable Change
Developmental History

In this section, we identify the circumstances under which the LAC framework developed—the reasons why it came about, the context and forces that were considered during its initial development.

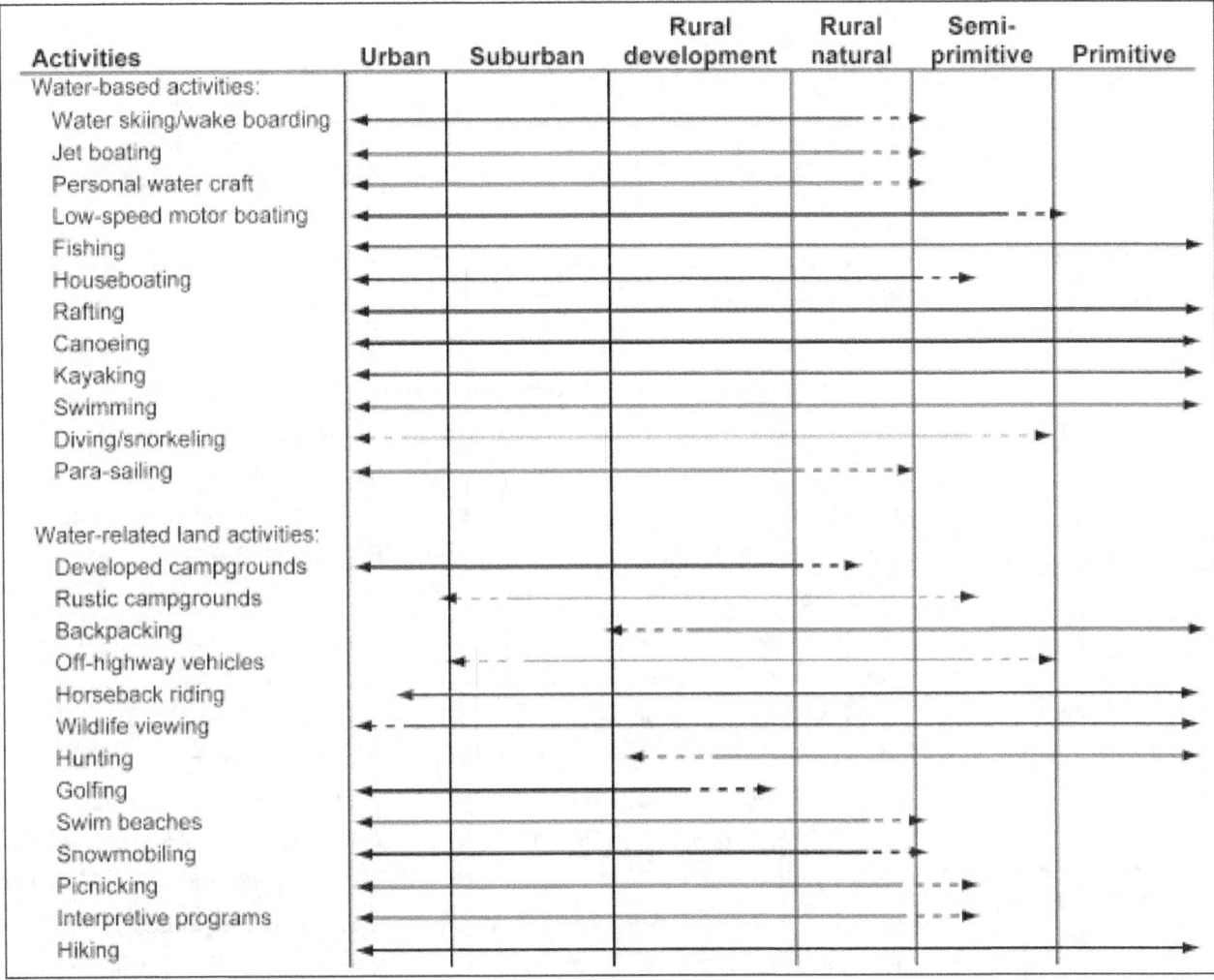

Figure 5—Example of acceptable activities in different water recreation opportunity classes. (Source: Haas et al. 2004).

The LAC was designed to respond to increasing calls to establish a recreation carrying capacity for designated wilderness. Although recreation carrying capacity is a concept that has a long presence in recreation management—dating back as early as the 1930s—it came to prominence in the 1960s and 1970s as a way of meeting provisions in the Wilderness Act of 1964 to provide "outstanding opportunities for solitude ..": too many people in a given wilderness at one time would obviously make it impossible to achieve this mandate (see section on Recreation Carrying Capacity for more detail; the basics of that history are repeated here). Beginning in the early 1970s with rapid rises in use of designated wilderness and increased use of wild and scenic rivers, managers were forced to wrestle with how they would protect the values they were charged with preserving. In 1972, managers of Grand Canyon National Park began limiting floating use of the Colorado River through the Park. This technique was rapidly adopted by other river recreation managers, such that a short 5 years later, use limits (often termed carrying capacities) had been emplaced on many other river segments in the Western United States.

With growing recreational use and the dominance of applied fields of biology (forestry, wildlife management, range conservation) that often used the notion of carrying capacity to formulate strategies for managing animals, it was quite natural that these fields turned to this notion as they were forced to address the rising use of public lands for recreation. The concept of carrying capacity has played a dominant, if evolving role in range and wildlife management over the last century (Roe 1997), and thus its utility for managing recreation was never significantly questioned until Wagar's argument in the mid 1970s (Wagar 1974).

However, this experience was not always positive; indeed, limiting use on popular whitewater rivers has been the most controversial action public land recreation managers have ever taken. Use limits, again often termed "carrying capacities," frequently triggered protests, lawsuits, and civil disobedience with the concern often over how limited use opportunities would be allocated among private and commercial users. During the last 40 years, thousands of studies and technical reports examined the idea of a recreational carrying capacity, proposed actual capacities, or indicated that such capacities should be established. In most cases, the capacities established were simply limits on use that were based primarily on a previous year's use level. Despite the limited success of the search for what eventually came to be known as "magic numbers," managers, including those of terrestrial wilderness, continued to seek ways of limiting use. For a variety of reasons, limiting use was not achieving the goal of protecting the scarce resource and special experiences found in wilderness. Research demonstrated that the relationship between use level and the amount of biophysical and social impact was complex, nonlinear, and mitigated by a number of intervening variables.

Beginning in the late 1970s, managers began asking if there were not some process or approach that might be more efficient, more effective, and more scientifically sound in dealing with the consequences of increased use. The regulations promulgated in response to NFMA indicated that national forest managers should establish a recreation carrying capacity for designated wilderness. In addition, the 1978 General Authorities Act for units of the NPS required managers to establish a recreation carrying capacity for each unit. This legislation eventually prompted the

Research demonstrated that the relationship between use level and the amount of biophysical and social impact was complex, nonlinear, and mitigated by a number of intervening variables.

National Parks and Conservation Association to contract with researchers at the University of Maryland to derive a process that managers could use to meet this requirement. These two policy statements spurred the development of processes to address these needs.

Simultaneously, researchers, led by the Forest Service Wilderness Management Research Unit, who often interacted with managers, were finding that solitude was neither the most important dimension of a wilderness experience sought nor was it necessarily linearly (e.g., Stankey 1972) related to use levels. Research was also showing that the biophysical consequences of recreational use in wilderness was also not linearly related to use levels (fig. 6). In an early statement, Frissell and Stankey (1972) indicated that recreational use of wilderness occurred within a dynamic ecological context; that change in natural conditions was always occurring (regardless of the presence of recreation), and that recreation-induced changes occurred but within this context. They extended this discussion to changes in the social domain. The problem, as they saw it, was identifying the recreation-induced change and determining how much of that change was acceptable in the context of wilderness.

Beginning in the late 1970s, a number of scientists associated with this research work unit and the University of Montana collaborated on formalizing the underlying concept of acceptable change and translating this concept into a planning system, eventually termed LAC. This planning system was published in 1985 (Stankey et al. 1985) concurrent with its first implementation in the Bob Marshall Wilderness Complex (BMWC) of Montana (McCool et al. 1985, Stankey et al. 1984). This implementation was articulated as an amendment to the Flathead, Lewis and Clark, Helena, and Lolo National Forests plans as required by NFMA.

Simultaneous with the development of LAC, the University of Maryland scientific team developed a process termed Visitor Impact Management (VIM) (Graefe et al. 1990). The process was similar to the LAC, but it was not the same. Important distinctions were in the area of scale (VIM was oriented toward sites, LAC to areas) and procedural location of the inventory step, and an explicit step stating "define the cause of the problem." However, VIM was never widely implemented, partly because it was developed outside the normal NPS planning process and partly because there was little managerial collaboration.[4]

---

[4] For these reasons, we do not explicitly cover VIM in this paper.

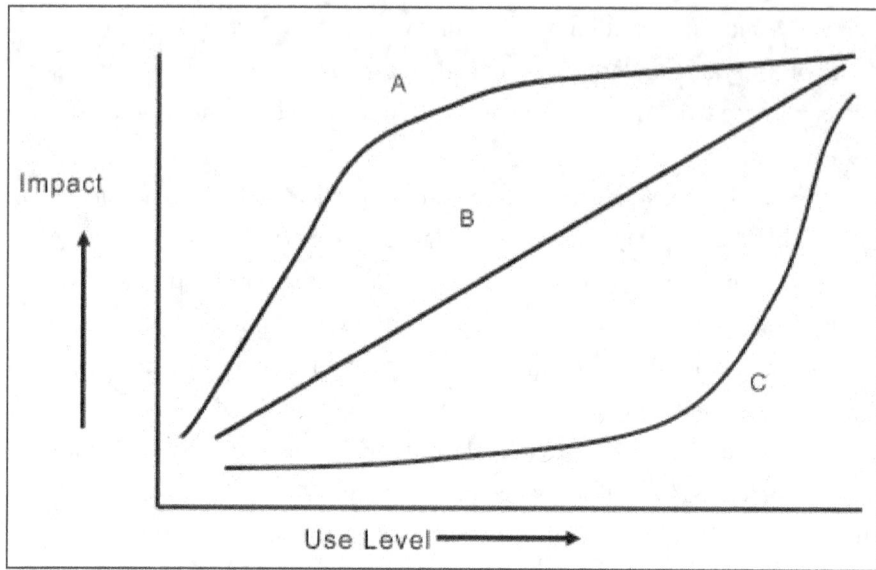

Figure 6—Three potential curves describing the relationship between use and impact. Research shows that these relationships are best depicted by curve A, suggesting that an inherent carrying capacity does not exist.

At this time, there was an increasing tendency to view humans as an agent of disturbance, and that such disturbances led to negative impacts. This viewpoint was particularly significant in areas managed by the NPS under the 1916 act to protect the "scenery therein" and allow enjoyment to the extent it did not impair park values. Because landscape ecology as a field was being developed at this time, humans were often considered a disturbance agent, just as other processes, such as fire or insects were.

By the mid 1990s, the NPS was under increasing pressure to meet the General Authorities Act mandate and began to consider how it could take the concepts and processes developed in VIM and LAC and apply it to its own backcountry and Wilderness within the context of its General Management Plan (GMP) process. They are the guiding policy and management document for units of the NPS. The NPS felt that the GMP process was alright, but could be informed by LAC and VIM. The outcome is a process termed "Visitor Experience and Resource Protection" or VERP (Hof and Lime 1997). Like LAC, VERP includes indicators, standards, zoning, management actions, and monitoring. However, it places inventory relatively early in the process, whereas LAC has it later.

The VERP process was initially tested in Arches National Park, modified and then implemented in several others, such as Glacier and Mount Rainier National Parks in the late 1990s and early in the 21st century (see USDI National Park Service 1997 for a manual on VERP implementation). The original implementation had been weak on public engagement; but this was corrected in later versions. However, the implementation of VERP has been mixed—identification of indicators and standards has generally not been included in the GMP process, whereas for more specific resources (e.g., rivers) it has been used in a more complete form (see following section on VERP).

Other manifestations of LAC were also developed in the 1990s, specifically the Tourism Optimization and Management Model in Australia (Manidis Roberts 1997) and the Protected Area Visitor Impact Model—the latter has been proposed to deal with the alleged complexity of LAC, but its applications in the real world are not documented in the literature (Farrell and Marion 2002). These other approaches used LAC as the central framework but adapted it to meet some other specific criteria contexts.

Each of these frameworks shares similarities in that they focus on identifying and managing visitor-induced impacts more than providing, in a more assertive manner, recreation opportunities. They each rely on goals and objectives and also include indicators and standards in their implementation.

Description of Limits of Acceptable Change

There are two descriptions of the LAC—one is a conceptual definition, and the other describes it as a step-by-step planning process. At the conceptual level, LAC was viewed as the amount of human-induced change that was acceptable in a wilderness setting, oriented principally around recreational uses (Stankey et al. 1985). Natural and human-induced change typifies wilderness and other similar environments; LAC is directed toward managing human-induced changes. Because low amounts of recreational use lead to disproportionately high amounts of impact, preventing impacts is not necessarily the issue, but managing them is.

The central question originally addressed by LAC was, "How much impact is acceptable and what strategies should be taken to avoid unacceptable impacts?" This question redefines the notion that drove early concerns about recreational use away from "How many is too many?" to understanding what is appropriate or acceptable and for whom. This question is much more closely aligned with agency legal mandates and policy direction than that suggested by a carrying capacity approach (see earlier discussion about carrying capacity).

LAC is directed toward managing human-induced changes.

More recently, this definition of LAC has been generalized to situations where two (or more) goals are in conflict. One goal is viewed as having higher priority or greater importance than another, but there is a willingness to compromise on that goal so that the other goal may be attained (Cole and Stankey 1997). In wilderness and backcountry situations, for example, one goal may be sustaining the natural conditions and processes that give rise to the area's value, and a secondary goal may be providing recreational access. The first goal is termed the "ultimately constraining goal," but can be compromised somewhat in order for (the second goal) recreational access to be permitted. Natural conditions are allowed to be degraded somewhat by recreation, but only until they have reached the limit of what is socially permissible. At that point, recreational access is limited in order to protect the principal or higher priority goal. This newer, more generalized definition of LAC allows managers to more easily transfer the concept to areas other than designated wilderness and backcountry situations.

At the practical level, LAC is implemented through a 9-step process described below (see fig. 7), although more recently, a recommendation has been made to expand this into 10 steps (McCool and Cole 1997a), adding as a first step an explicit statement of area goals and values. Importantly, the steps act together as a system. Consequently attempts to "short-cut" the system by removing or changing the sequence of steps are likely to result in failure.

What follows is a description of the steps involved in the LAC process. With each step, we first briefly describe the step and follow with a rationale for the step.

1. Identify area issues and concerns—Citizens and managers meet to identify what special features or qualities within the area require attention, what management problems or concerns have to be dealt with, what issues the public considers important in the area's management, and what role the area fills in both a regional and national context. This step encourages a better understanding of the wilderness resource, a general concept of how the resource should be managed, and a focus on principal management issues. The LAC is very much driven not only by legislative mandates (in the case of wilderness) to protect the values for which the area was established, but also by the issues or challenges that threaten these values.

This step is important not only in identifying these issues, but also for reaching agreement with affected publics that these issues need to be resolved through the LAC process. Issues such as outfitter allocation, horse and trail management, threatened and endangered species, and opportunities for solitude were identified as important in the BMWC. If issues are defined as barriers to reaching goals for an

Figure 7—The Limits of Acceptable Change planning framework. The framework was designed as a system; eliminating or changing the sequence of steps may adversely affect the ability of the system to address the issues it was designed to assist with.

area, this step is essential to understanding what stands in the way of achieving those goals. Management actions are eventually developed that address these issues.

2. Define and describe wilderness recreation opportunity classes—Any wilderness area contains a diversity of physical-biological features, use levels, evidence of recreation and other human uses, and opportunities for wilderness experiences. The type of management needed will also differ throughout an area. Opportunity classes describe subdivisions or zones of wilderness where different resource, social and managerial conditions will be maintained. These classes represent a way of defining a range of diverse conditions within the wilderness. And although diversity is the objective, note that the conditions found in all cases must be consistent with the area's designation as wilderness. The definition of opportunity classes is not an excuse to maintain conditions inappropriate in a wilderness.

This step, one of the most difficult in the LAC process, describes the **current** diversity of conditions. The notion of an opportunity class initially was derived from the ROS planning framework (see that section) and is designed to identify what diversity of opportunities **currently** exist and then eventually explicate what opportunities **should** exist. This step is located at this point in the framework to make explicit the need to consider diversity and agree on more specific goals and values than may have been adopted or discussed in step 1. By focusing discussion of what opportunities exist at this step, managers and the public are laying a foundation for what indicators of biophysical or social conditions may be needed later. They are establishing a rationale for any re-allocation of what opportunity classes should be maintained and where within the wilderness.

In step 2, general descriptions of the resource, social, and managerial conditions appropriate to each class are developed. For example, table 6 shows the resource and social settings in each of four opportunity classes that existed in the BMWC in the early 1980s, ranging from pristine conditions to one typified by the relatively more visible impacts of human use. These classes defined the range of conditions that existed but did not involve specific allocations of land. Allocations of land to specific opportunity classes occur in step 6. However the descriptions of these classes ultimately will serve as management objectives for specific areas of the wilderness.

In the initial application in the BMWC, there was often confusion and as a result unnecessary debate about the title of the four opportunity classes that were described. Eventually, a decision was made **not** to provide a title, but rather label the opportunity classes with Roman numerals (e.g., I, II, III, and IV) thus avoiding the meaning of inherently value-laden terms such as "primitive," which also tended to conflict with manager and public understanding of the meaning of wilderness.

3. Select indicators of biophysical and social conditions—Indicators are specific elements of the biophysical and social setting selected to represent (or to be "indicative of") the conditions deemed appropriate and acceptable in each opportunity class. Because it is impossible to measure the condition of and change in every biophysical and social feature in a wilderness, only a few indicators need to be selected. Examples would include amount of bare ground at campsites or average number of other groups encountered per day. Indicators should be easy to measure quantitatively and be related to the conditions specified by the opportunity classes.

Because it is impossible to measure the condition of and change in every biophysical and social feature in a wilderness, only a few indicators need to be selected.

Indicators are an important part of the LAC process because their values reflect the overall conditions found throughout an opportunity class. It is important to understand that an individual indicator might not adequately depict the condition of a particular area. It is the "bundle" of indicators that is used to monitor an area. Indicators also allow establishing quantitative standards of acceptable conditions (which are developed in step 5). The tabulation below shows the indicators selected in the BMWC.

Biophysical	Social
Forage utilization	Number of other campsites occupied within continuous sight or sound
Campsite condition	Number of trail encounters per day
Density of campsites	

In general, useful indicators are those that are quantitative (eliminates ambiguity), reliable (differences from one period or place to another are due to real changes not measurement error), sensitive to change (in order to measure effectiveness of management actions), administratively feasible (are not costly to implement or require highly skilled individuals), and related to important objectives and issues (to provide feedback on how well actions aimed at improving or sustaining conditions are effective).

As a planning framework, LAC often is confused with this step. For example, backcountry rangers frequently report doing LAC indicator monitoring—when they are actually measuring certain variables related to the biophysical condition of a campsite, such as area of barren core. Measuring these variables out of context of the framework may be something that is needed, but is not the same as implementing LAC. A completed LAC process may require monitoring of these variables, but simply doing that and none of the other steps can hardly be termed LAC.

Managers frequently want to use indicators (and the associated standards) developed in other places to save themselves time and work. Although the LAC framework is a generic process, the specifics are highly place, issue, and goal specific. The **process** of developing indicators itself is a learning exercise that is fundamental to creating a better understanding of an area, the issues confronting it, and the appropriateness of management actions.

4. Inventory existing biophysical and social conditions—Inventories can be a time-consuming and expensive part of planning. In the LAC framework, the inventory is guided by the indicators selected in step 3 and therefore is conducted not as a first step, but only after there has been deliberation about what biophysical attributes, social conditions, and managerial actions are important and why. The inventory stage would spatially identify the value of indicators (such as the location of campsites at varying impact levels). Other factors, such as bridges, lookout towers, outfitter base camps, and critical habitat, may also be inventoried, particularly if these factors are important for visitor use and impact management actions.

The information generated by the inventory will be helpful later when the consequences of various alternatives are being evaluated and to identify where and with what priority management actions should occur. Without the inventory, managers would have little idea of the potential consequences on various values and conditions and would not completely understand where and what actions should be implemented. The inventory data are mapped so that both the condition and location of the indicators are known. The inventory provides a measure of the indicators' existing condition throughout the area, as well as a database from which managers can formulate the standards for each indicator in each opportunity class.

5. Specify standards for biophysical and social conditions in each opportunity class—We identify the range of conditions for each indicator considered appropriate and acceptable for each opportunity class. By defining those conditions in measurable terms, we provide the basis for establishing a distinctive, diverse, and agreeable range of wilderness opportunities. Standards serve to define the "limits of acceptable change." They are the maximum permissible conditions that will be allowed in a specific opportunity class; they are not necessarily objectives or desirable conditions. Typically, each opportunity class would have a distinctive, quantitative standard for each indicator, generally along a continuum that reflects the increasing primitiveness of the desired conditions.

The inventory data in step 4 play an important role in setting standards. The standards defining the range of acceptable conditions in each opportunity class need to be realistic and attainable; however, they should not necessarily mimic existing conditions. When standards mimic existing conditions, the result is to eliminate areas and conditions that need restoration or other action; by definition, these areas are within the limit of acceptable change.

Standards play a critical role of indicating when restoration, enhancement, or other management actions might be needed. For example, if conditions are well within the limit established by a standard, there may be little need for management action. However, as conditions approach the standard, managers would want to implement actions to prevent violations of the standard from occurring. The use of standards also provides an unambiguous statement as to what conditions in wilderness are acceptable or unacceptable. The comparison of monitoring data (step 9) with standards provides the public with assurances that conditions are acceptable for designated wilderness, and an explicit rationale for why, where and when certain management actions may be needed. Standards are the critical component of the LAC process; they reflect a set of judgments and agreements about what conditions will be acceptable, given a desire to recreate in wilderness. The question of whose judgments count in developing standards remains an important one. In the original implementation of LAC in the Bob Marshall Wilderness, a variety of publics were directly involved in negotiating appropriate standards, with scientists and managers helping identify the consequences of alternative standards. Lucas (1985) provided important information on use and intergroup encounter levels in this discussion.

Are standards "red lights" or warning "yellow lights"? The former suggests standards are "hard" and should not be violated if at all possible. The latter indicates that standards are "soft" and only suggest where, when, and what actions may be taken. If standards are soft, then managers are not necessarily required to take action. In many organizations, such soft standards would be used as a reason to avoid controversial decisions. Hard standards are more likely to contain real meaning.

6. Identify alternative opportunity class allocations reflecting area-wide issues and concerns and existing biophysical and social conditions—Most wildernesses could be managed in several different ways and still retain their basic wilderness qualities. In step 6, we begin to identify some of these alternatives. Using information from step 1 (area values, issues, and concerns) and step 4 (inventory of existing conditions), managers and citizens can begin to explore how well different opportunity class allocations meet varying interests, concerns, and values. Step 6 is prescriptive: it involves mapping and thus allocating the opportunity classes identified in step 2. Not all such opportunity classes may actually be used; a group may decide to narrow or broaden the range of opportunities offered. The different alternatives may allocate differing proportions of the wilderness to opportunity classes, thus reflecting varying philosophies of how a wilderness could be managed.

Critical to development of the alternatives is a statement of philosophy or purpose for each alternative, such as "this alternative seeks to maximize the availability of primitive recreation opportunities." This statement sends a clear signal that resulting opportunity class allocations will reflect the purpose.

Step 6 plays an essential role in the LAC process. It explicitly separates in time and sequence descriptive components of planning (e.g., step 2) from the prescriptive. It provides the opportunity to examine different pathways to protecting a particular wilderness. It serves as the foundation for step 7 and for identifying environmental (social and biophysical) consequences of alternatives (step 8), thus providing information useful in environmental assessments.

For example, in the BMWC planning effort, one alternative allocated a large proportion of the area to those opportunity classes in which impact is least acceptable. However, another alternative gives greater emphasis to those opportunity classes where higher impact levels are acceptable. Yet another alternative featured maintenance of the status quo. Each alternative thus carries with it implications for the social, environmental, and managerial costs and benefits.

7. Identify management actions for each alternative—The alternative allocations proposed in step 6 are only the first step in the process of developing a preferred alternative. In addition to the kinds of conditions that would be achieved, both managers and citizens need to know what management actions will be needed to achieve the desired conditions. In a sense, step 7 requires an analysis of the costs, broadly defined, that will be imposed by each alternative. For example, many people might find attractive an alternative that calls for restoration of much of the area to a pristine character. However, such an alternative might necessitate introduction of strict use rationing, prohibition of horses, and closure of some areas. In light of such costs, the alternative might not seem as attractive.

Step 7 provides a measure of what it will take to move the area from its existing condition to that desired. As such it is an important component of making informed decisions about the tradeoffs needed for access to wilderness as well as to restore or enhance certain desired conditions.

Management actions may include information, education, campsite closure and rehabilitation, increased enforcement of regulations, restrictions on party size, use limits, length of stay limits, and so on. The action proposed for a specific area differs according to the opportunity class and intensity of the problem as defined by comparing existing conditions with the standards developed.

8. Evaluate and select a preferred alternative—With the various costs and benefits before them, citizens and managers can proceed to evaluate the various alternatives, and the managing authority will then select a preferred alternative. Evaluation must take many factors into consideration, but examples would include the responsiveness of each alternative to the issues and concerns identified in step 1, the management requirements identified in step 7, and typical evaluation criteria such as environmental impacts, costs of implementation, distributional consequences, and so on. In addition, a rule describing how the choice will be made among alternatives needs to be developed. It is important that the criteria involved in the evaluation process and their relative importance be made explicit and available for public review.

The evaluation process would be similar to an environmental analysis, and might be incorporated into it. This step is important because it allows managers to disclose the costs associated with wilderness protection and recreational use, explicitly identify the criteria by which the analysis will be conducted, and develop a rule by which the preferred alternative will be chosen. The process of deliberating these items in a public venue produces learning and a more informed decision.

9. Implement actions and monitor conditions—With an alternative selected, the necessary management actions (if any) are put into effect and a monitoring program instituted. The monitoring program focuses on the indicators selected in step 3 and compares their condition with those identified in the standards. If conditions are not improving, the intensity of the management effort might need to be increased or new actions implemented. In this way, monitoring becomes an integrated component of management, not an expensive and optional "add-on" as it is often perceived in protected area management. Monitoring suggests the effectiveness of management in attaining or sustaining goals established earlier, identifies any unanticipated consequences (e.g., limiting use in one area may lead to it increasing someplace else), and leads to management that is more adaptive and responds to new issues and problems. As a result, incorporation of a monitoring protocol means that new job descriptions are written: some old tasks are dropped, some new ones are added, and some existing ones are still done, but with new reasons. Implementation of LAC then means that some significant changes must occur in the organization, otherwise it will fail.

Monitoring suggests the effectiveness of management in attaining or sustaining goals established earlier.

How frequently and where should indicators be monitored? This is a key question and how one responds to it affects the success of implementation. Monitoring need not require lists of variables to be measured frequently and everywhere; indeed, in the BMWC, only nine variables were identified and most were prescribed to be measured on a less than annual basis. It is important to understand the character of the system being monitored as well as the quality and quantity of information needed to understand the effectiveness of management actions. A monitoring plan detailing and defining indicators, their measurement, and how the resulting information will be displayed, evaluated, and used is essential to both minimizing costs and maximizing the utility of the monitoring effort.

In summary, LAC-based (sometimes referred to as indicator-based) approaches to management of recreation were largely developed out of failures to establish a recreation carrying capacity in wilderness and wilderness-like settings. When limits on use were implemented (often termed a carrying capacity), such limits also often failed to address the underlying reason for the limit. Experience with LAC has been most widespread; some adaptations of it have been made, each with limited success and applications.

Key Concepts and Premises

A critical concept for the LAC process is the notion of **acceptability**, which we now have come to understand as an assessment of the costs and benefits of a particular condition or management action and a decision that the costs involved are worth the benefits. What is acceptable is differentiated from **preferred** conditions or actions, which may be defined as what is favored or desired without reference to costs or consequences. Although scientists and managers understood that it was important to find out what visitors and others with interest in wilderness preferred, providing those conditions was impossible given the multiplicity of goals, expectations, and demands on wilderness. Thus, researchers recommended managers consider identifying what conditions were acceptable.

The character of the relationship between use levels and resulting impacts influenced this recommendation as well (see fig. 6). Research on this relationship by Cole (e.g., 1995), Leung and Marion (e.g., 2000) in particular (dealing primarily with impacts in the biophysical domain) challenged the implicit assumption of carrying capacity that such relationships were not only predictable, but also were characterized by a "J-shaped" curve. A J-shaped curve would suggest an inherent carrying capacity. But the research suggested otherwise, thus indicating there was no use level where biophysical impacts could be prevented.

Much of the driving interest in addressing recreation in wilderness developed out of a concern that visitors would not be able to experience the "outstanding opportunities for solitude ..." mandated by the Wilderness Act. In short, designated wildernesses would be too crowded. The concept of **crowding** has been much researched in the recreation literature, and we define it here as an evaluative judgment of the use density experienced by a visitor. Crowding is the result of visitors applying some norm to the number of visitors they encounter during a visit and leading to a judgment that a place contains too many people (Stokols 1972). Because norms differ considerably from one person to another, and one setting to another based on a variety of factors, what one person feels is crowded, another may view as "just right." Crowding can be viewed as distinctly separate from the notion of **congestion,** which is more concerned with the density and physical interference of one user versus another. Thus, a setting may be congested but not crowded. Because concept of crowding reflects a normative judgment, it is often better to use the term **use density**, which is simply the number of visitors per unit area.

The LAC framework separates in time and sequence planning actions that are descriptive from those that are prescriptive. **Descriptive** actions depict a current situation or setting as it is, that is, they describe what is. **Prescriptive** actions describe what is desired or what should be. Thus, step 4 of LAC involves an inventory. Although the inventory eventually influences what might be (in the sense of what is practical and realistic), it should not be confused with what should be—the desired future state of a recreation setting.

The original implementation of the LAC framework in the Bob Marshall Wilderness Complex involved a citizen task force to work with managers in working through the framework. The citizen task force was critical to the initial success of this application. Using citizens allowed important information gaps to be filled as the dialog that developed acknowledged the legitimacy of experiential knowledge, tested the social acceptability of proposed actions, and developed ownership in the plan by citizens (Ashor and McCool 1984). This process is now known as **collaboration**—citizens, managers, and scientists working together to construct a consensus about a proposed course of action. Collaborative processes have become the hallmark of contemporary natural resource management. In the BMWC, the process was guided by the theory of transactive planning, which briefly stated is, dialog among those affected by a decision leads to social learning about the various dimensions of that decision, which then leads to societal action—agreement on what choice or alternative to pursue (Friedmann 1973).

The success of a technical planning framework such as LAC may be strongly linked to its implementation as a collaborative process. Not only does LAC structure the character of the discussion among those involved, it explicates the numerous **value judgments** (choices between value systems that are at least partially

> The success of a technical planning framework such as LAC may be strongly linked to its implementation as a collaborative process.

overlapping and partially competing) involved in public land recreation management. Three particularly important value judgments are made explicit by the LAC framework: (1) selecting and describing the purpose and goals for a particular place, (2) identifying and ranking issues and concerns to be addressed through the planning framework, and (3) setting standards for what is defined as acceptable or not acceptable conditions (Krumpe and McCool 1997).

The LAC planning framework eventually leads to the establishment of formalized standards of acceptable change. Such standards are applied to **indicators**—quantifiable variables that are monitored periodically and systematically over time and space that reflect a particular set of social or biophysical conditions. Indicators are combined with **standards,** which are defined as a formalized, explicit statement of the maximum acceptable human-induced change in an indicator. Each indicator has an associated standard. A standard is the limit of acceptable change. Generally, the most useful standards are quantifiable statements of the least acceptable condition for an opportunity class. Thus, a standard for campsite conditions may be written as "no more than 1,000 square feet of bare soil" or "an 80-percent probability that a person will not encounter more than 2 other groups camped within sight or sound." Such standards clearly communicate what conditions are acceptable and which are not. They reflect, as noted above, a value judgment about the tradeoffs between recreational access and protection of biophysical or social conditions.

Another significant concept used in the LAC planning system is the notion of **opportunity classes**. An opportunity class is an area within wilderness that has similar biophysical, social, and managerial conditions; opportunity classes are differentiated from each other by the standards that have been defined for indicators. The use of the concept of opportunity class was a direct recognition that even within wilderness, variability of biophysical and social conditions is inevitable and may be desirable, and reflects a lineage to the ROS. Opportunity classes are distinguished not only by their descriptions but also by the presence of different standards.

A final significant component of the LAC system is its emphasis on **monitoring.** Monitoring may be defined as the periodic and systematic measurement of key indicator variables in such a way that results are assessed and evaluated in the context of management objectives and actions. In LAC, monitoring was recognized as an essential component that forces evaluation of management actions. Such evaluations had rarely been conducted with respect to implementation of use limit policies.

The core driving component of LAC is the conflict between two objectives of wilderness management: providing a pristine environment and access to recreational opportunities (Cole and Stankey 1997). The LAC represents a process where one of these competing objectives is defined as not being compromised, but another that may be. For the one that is compromised, a set of standards is employed. Thus, LAC represents a process to make tradeoffs among competing objectives, the heart of wilderness management. In the words of Cole and Stankey: "In the recreation application, when the maximum acceptable limit of resource degradation is reached, no more degradation is allowed, and recreation use is restricted as much as necessary."

Implementation Requirements

To implement the LAC framework, agencies need to address three questions:

1. Does the agency hold the commitment to complete the entire process, including engaging the public?
2. Does the agency hold or can it obtain the technical skills needed to work through the framework?
3. What types of technical biophysical and social information are needed?

In this section, we introduce the requirements needed to successfully address these questions.

Agency commitment—
Of primary importance is the agency's will or commitment to completing the process. The LAC has often been criticized by managers and scientists as complicated and lengthy (Farrell and Marion 2002). Although we dispute the notion that this framework is any more complicated than any other framework concerning natural resource stewardship, we acknowledge that the framework does reflect the complexity of issues, values, and problems confronting public land recreation managers. Agencies frequently respond to the perceived complicated character of the framework by desiring to "short cut" it, eliminate steps, forego the public engagement process that has become fundamental to its success, or pass the monitoring phase off to other divisions within an organization.

This approach can cause problems. In the messy situations confronting recreation managers today, learning and consensus building are critical elements of building a successful plan—one that has ownership of the affected publics and can be implemented. Each step involved in LAC has a learning function, for agency

> In the messy situations confronting recreation managers today, learning and consensus building are critical elements of building a successful plan.

managers, scientists, and members of the public. Eliminating steps impacts this learning. For example, managers often seek to adopt indicators and standards developed for other areas. But those indicators and standards are site specific and reflect not only the conditions located at a specific area but also public preferences and notions of acceptability operative in that setting. Each was selected following substantial deliberation, debate, and decision processes that led to learning and consensus building. To adopt them in a different place in an attempt to save planning costs removes these important processes from that planning situation; the rationale for the selection of specific indicators and standards is not understood.

Public engagement is often viewed as an extra cost in planning. Agencies frequently lack the public facilitation skills needed. There are sometimes significant barriers for federal agencies, such as the 1972 Federal Advisory Committee Act (see discussion below). Under these conditions, there are no real incentives to engage the public. However, working through LAC without substantial public engagement means that value judgments are hidden, there will be little understanding of why certain decisions are made, and the social acceptability of proposed management will not be identified.

Sometimes agencies decide that development of indicators and appropriate monitoring protocols should be left to the managers that implement LAC. This compartmentalization of components has led to situations where processes have only been partly implemented, reinforcing the notion that monitoring is a costly "extra" in recreation planning. By compartmentalizing functions, managers themselves may have little ownership in the outcomes of the LAC framework, and thus little incentive to engage in monitoring. The monitoring may never be conducted, and thus one of the key strengths of the LAC framework—understanding the effectiveness of actions designed to meet specific standards—is lost.

Information requirements—
Like other planning systems, LAC requires a certain type of information for its implementation. Much of this information is technical in nature: inventories of appropriate biophysical and social conditions, locations and descriptions of key facilities, campsites, trails, roads, vegetation, habitat, threatened and endangered species, and so on. In addition, knowledge of recreation use patterns, impacts, preferences for desired and/or acceptable conditions, and attitudes toward potential management actions are helpful to completion of the framework. This information is then analyzed, synthesized, and displayed by using contemporary planning tools

such as a geographic information system. Finally, because LAC focuses on judgments of what conditions are acceptable or appropriate, some means of gaining this information from visitors, those with interest in wilderness, scientists, and managers is needed. Thus, the agency must have the capability to acquire this information and translate it into practice in a public setting.

In one sense, this may seem like a lot of information; indeed it is. Not all the above may be required in any given situation, but much of it will be. Thus, the decision to use LAC requires agencies to also commit to gathering the needed data.

Needed skills—

Two fundamental skill sets are required to implement LAC. First, planners involved must hold the technical analysis and procedural skills needed for any planning framework, as noted in chapter 3. This would include knowledge and familiarity with the agency's formalized planning process and how to integrate LAC into it, mapping and data display, and an ability to interpret the meaning of biophysical and social data. In this case, planners should also hold a basic understanding of recreation or wilderness management; recreation user needs, preferences, and norms (and how to use this information); and how recreation integrates with other public land values.

Second, planners need public involvement and meeting facilitation skills. That is, planners need to understand the basics of public meeting management (such as selecting a venue, facilitating interaction between and among members of the public and agency personnel, etc.) as well as negotiating, consensus building, and conflict management basics. These skills are the foundation upon which the public engagement process can proceed in a timely and constructive manner. These skills are fundamental to achieving processes that are open and deliberative, as observed in chapter 3.

This is a great diversity of skills. Most individuals will not hold all of them. Thus, agencies will need to consider how they acquire and manage these skills and the costs and benefits of both using them and not using them.

Assessment of Experience With LAC

In this section, we provide an assessment of the LAC framework by discussing strengths and weaknesses, barriers to implementation, and the lessons learned through application. To set the stage for this evaluation, we first discuss, briefly, the initial application of LAC to give the reader an idea of how such a framework can be implemented.

The first application of LAC occurred contemporaneously with the latter stages of its technical development and was focused on the Bob Marshall Wilderness Complex (three juxtaposed wildernesses: the Bob Marshall, Great Bear, and Scapegoat located in northwestern Montana). The complex is administered by four national forests through five ranger districts and lies astride the Continental Divide. It includes about 1,482,632 acres (600 000 hectares), 1,500 miles of trail, and well over 1,000 identified campsites. An extensive amount of outfitting occurs centered primarily, but not solely, around big game hunting. An estimated 20,000 visitors entered the complex annually in the mid to late 1980s when the LAC process was first being applied there.

The LAC-based planning effort was generated as a result of broad managerial and public dissatisfaction with a previous recreation management plan that had little public acceptability or ownership. The wilderness staff officer working with the forest supervisor on the Flathead National Forest (which eventually was designated the "lead" on the planning effort), decided that a new approach to planning was needed, both in its technical aspects as well as in how the public was engaged in the planning process itself. Thus, it asked the scientists at the then Wilderness Management Research Work Unit at the Rocky Mountain Research Station (succeeded by the current Aldo Leopold Wilderness Research Institute) to help managers apply LAC. At the same time, managers decided to engage the public in new ways (see Stankey et al. 1984, Stokes 1990) through the formation of an "LAC Task Force." The task force involved about 35 members of the public and included outfitters, hikers, advocates, horseback users, as well as managers and scientists. It met one to three times a year beginning in 1982. The plan was completed in 1987. Although the task force was formally disbanded in the early 1990s because of concerns developed out of the Federal Advisory Committee Act, the Forest Service still meets annually with the public about management issues. During the development of the plan, the task force went through each of the nine steps of LAC in this public setting (often other members of the public attended meetings to observe and provide input). Agency managers and scientists served as technical advisors. Line managers made decisions on issues in this setting as they could. Disputes were handled by a consensus process (this does not mean that there was unanimous opinion, only that members agreed to go along with a decision they did not like). The plan was amended to each of the four forest plans in 1987 following a formal environmental assessment.

The model for the public engagement process was Friedmann's theory of transactive planning (1973). Briefly stated, this theory proposes that dialog between planners and affected publics is needed to overcome a gap in understanding each others' language (with the gap being a major barrier to effective planning). Such dialog would lead to mutual learning, not only about the content or subject of the planning effort but also about planning processes and the individuals involved. Mutual learning would then lead to societal guidance, a set of decisions that would be needed to resolve the particular subject of the planning effort. In the Bob Marshall case, this approach structured the overall planning process as well as individual meetings. For example, scientists were often invited to present research results, particularly research concerning social and biophysical impacts of recreation. Public members were encouraged to discuss what they felt were the unique and important social values of the wilderness. Managers often indicated what actions or approaches would be administratively feasible and/or legal.

Most task force members felt a deep sense of ownership about the plan when it was completed, lobbied for funding for its implementation, and often have participated in informal enforcement of its provisions. Thus, this initial application combined an innovative technical planning process with intimate public engagement (fig. 8). These two were weaved together such that LAC provided the overall framework for engaging the public (e.g., meetings were organized around the steps), and the public engagement provided the kind of ownership and social acceptability needed to implement a plan in a contentious social context.

Following its initial application in the Bob Marshall Wilderness (Stankey et al. 1984), many areas quickly adopted the process, such as the Selway-Bitterroot Wilderness, the Beartrap Canyon portion of the Lee Metcalf Wilderness, the South Fork of the Snake River Area of Critical Environmental Concern, and so on. By 1990, at least 23 wilderness planning efforts were using LAC (McCoy et al. 1995). By 1995, this number had grown to 50 just within the National Forest System. Other efforts were underway in Australia, Malaysia, and Belize.

The relatively rapid and widespread use of LAC was probably attributable to several factors. Like ROS, LAC was a collaborative effort, with most of the principal scientists deeply involved with managers, particularly those in the Bob Marshall Wilderness. This involvement helped with the design of the process, and the presence of scientists serving as "consultants" facilitated the initial application. Second, the process used familiar concepts of an opportunity spectrum and zoning. Many wilderness managers had applied ROS in the past, and thus this component

Most task force members felt a deep sense of ownership about the plan when it was completed.

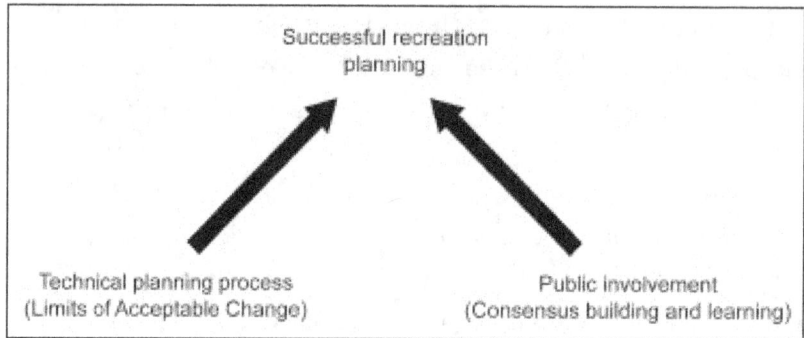

Figure 8—Successful planning in contentious situations depends on two processes that occur simultaneously: technical planning and public engagement. Each may be viewed as a necessary but not sufficient condition.

was familiar to them. New aspects of wilderness planning, such as indicators and standards, were relatively easy to understand within the context of the process, and managers could see some parallels between LAC and the forest planning process that was being implemented at a similar point in time. The LAC was also based on the science of the time, such as the acknowledged nonlinear association between use and impact. Planners using LAC also had recognized that a carrying capacity approach had not worked in other areas. The public appreciated the involvement of scientists and the give and take of discussions in meetings.

Strengths and Weaknesses

As a planning framework, LAC has a number of strengths. Foremost among these strengths is its explicitness. We've noted earlier that recreation management involves a number of value judgments—choices among competing expressions of public preferences. The LAC framework forces the consideration of these choices and judgments explicitly, that is, they are observable and trackable to others. The logic pathway (the series of steps in LAC) is visible to any who inspect it. Any inconsistencies in decisions from one step to another are quickly exposed. This is an advantage to both technical planning staff who can see how assumptions and statements earlier in the process influence decisions later in the process and to the public who want to understand how certain decisions are made given particular starting points. In sum, the process is open and understandable. These characteristics should mean that decisions are defendable because the logic flow can be tracked from one step to another.

A second strength is that LAC is based on scientifically developed principles and concepts, particularly with respect to management of recreational uses and values. Thus, it is an example of application of the best science possible to inform management decisions. And although LAC represents a scientifically based process, the outcomes of the process are only informed, not decided, by science. The LAC, although a traditional technical planning process, has been applied as an open, inclusive process where scientific knowledge is integrated with managerial expertise and local and experiential knowledge.

Third, LAC represents a systematic, rational process where the flow of information and experience from one step to another is easy to understand, efficient, and useful. Although some may feel the framework is complicated, when looking at LAC step by step, one can quickly grasp not only the logic behind each step but the sequence as well. As a systematic process, it is consistent from one setting to another, thus creating better citizen and manager understanding of an approach to decisionmaking. Adaptability is also a significant attribute in that monitoring is a component of the LAC framework. By building monitoring into the framework (and implementing the whole framework), changes in management can occur given the learning that comes through systematic monitoring and evaluation of conditions. This gives LAC the probability of being a highly effective framework, given organizational will to implement it.

A fourth strength is that the framework focuses on on-the-ground conditions— real situations, real places, real issues. This focus goes beyond maps of different opportunity classes to include a better understanding of spatial relationships that integrate inventory data, goals, and standards. This provides guidance as to what should be done in any given situation and helps create a better understanding of the spatial consequences of management actions. This provides appeal not only to managers but to the public as well.

Several weaknesses or criticisms have developed out of the applications of LAC. First, LAC is often viewed as too complicated and costly for most managers to implement.

The initial applications of LAC combined public task forces with technical planning. However, judicial and administrative interpretations of the Federal Advisory Committee Act—which limited federal planning teams to full-time federal employees unless a specific exemption was granted by General Services Administration—dampened the use of public task forces. The task force had been the central organizing feature of several planning efforts, including the Bob Marshall, Selway-Bitterroot, and the Bear Trap Canyon.

In 1997, McCool and Cole (1997a, 1997b) organized an assessment of LAC. The assessment involved both scientists and managers. The outcome of the assessment was (1) a recommendation to add a more explicit step at the beginning of the process to recognize the values of a specific wilderness, (2) recognition that public engagement was central to successful wilderness management, and (3) a broader or more fundamental description of LAC and the conditions under which it could be applied. The principal weaknesses of LAC that have been identified are its (1) alleged complexity, (2) a focus on the "negative" aspects of recreational use of wilderness, and (3) its inability to arrive at specific answers to recreationally induced problems. These weaknesses are more operational than systemic in nature, indicating that they can be addressed successfully through relatively minor changes.

Lessons Learned

1. Technical and public processes need to work in concert—In contentious settings, which typify many public land recreation situations, public engagement, often now termed "collaborative planning" is necessary. But so is the technical planning process of identifying goals, developing alternatives, selecting a preferred alternative, implementation, and monitoring. Both processes are needed (see fig. 8). The technical process provides the systematic, step-by-step process required to ensure the application of the best science available and to structure the public engagement process. Public engagement is essential to developing the consensus needed to support action in both technical management and political arenas— without consensus, funding and other support needed for implementation are not forthcoming. Learning is also a fundamental requirement in contentious and uncertain situations. Public engagement allows groups and individuals to gain a better appreciation of the complexities of public land management, learn about each other, and learn about process. When scientists and managers also "sit at the table," learning occurs for all groups.

Public engagement is essential to developing the consensus needed to support action in both technical management and political arenas

2. Expectations of the role of the public must be clear to all parties—In intimate public engagement, the role of the public needs to be discussed and clarified. Is the public to only comment on the initiatives of the agency? Is the public to help develop alternatives? Are decisions made with the full participation of the public? Here, the classic Arnstein's (1969) ladder of public participation might serve as a useful framework in addressing expectations. The higher up the ladder, the more involved the public is in the planning and decisionmaking process. Clarifying expectations at the beginning of the planning process will help avoid confusion and controversy at all stages, from determining the planning process and rules of conduct to how consensus will be reached.

3. Establish opportunities for dialog—Within contentious situations, dialog is fundamental to progress, learning, consensus building, and social action. Numerous and diverse opportunities for dialog among members of the public and between publics and the agency should be created. This includes using a variety of small and large group meeting techniques (e.g., nominal group, specific planning tasks), breaks, field trips, presentations by members of the public, and so on. Such opportunities allow people to discuss the content of the plan but also engage in the "small talk" that is fundamental to healthy interpersonal relationships.

4. Planning is negotiation; participants must be able to speak for those they represent—In many respects, a plan is a negotiated, socially acceptable agreement between the public that provides the funding and political support for an agency, and the agency which is mandated to meet certain legislative, but publicly developed, requirements. Plans must be socially and politically acceptable, or they cannot be implemented. Not all members of the public can or want to participate in a task force or other type of setting. Thus, planning is conducted by representatives of groups, stakeholders, or value systems. To negotiate, discuss issues, and construct consensus, these representatives must have the authority to speak and develop agreements for these groups. Managers and planners participating in or facilitating such public engagement processes must ensure that representatives do have such authority.

5. Bringing people in late can make problems—Construction of consensus requires that certain conditions be met: the problem definition is shared, agreement that the problem can be resolved through public deliberation, the process includes all affected interests, participants will be able to accept or "live with" results, the agency has "permission" to act, and that knowledge about the planning issue is distributed equally among participants (McCool et al. 2000). For these conditions to be met, all participants in engagement processes such as task forces must be involved from the beginning. Participants brought in later as different needs arise operate at a disadvantage: they may have dissimilar perceptions or definitions of the planning issue, they may be unfamiliar with the planning process, they may not have developed the interpersonal relationships important to communication within the group setting, or they may not hold the same knowledge about the issue as other participants. To give latecomers equal footing, the process would have to be stopped so other members of the group could educate them.

6. Uncertainty typifies recreation and wilderness management, particularly at larger spatial and temporal scales—Planning and public engagement processes must recognize this uncertainty and incorporate it into implementation strategies

Scientific and other forms of knowledge make claims about the relationships between causes and effects. Our knowledge is incomplete, however, and developed in contexts that often are different than what may occur in the future. Thus, decisionmaking occurs under conditions of uncertainty. Planning must proceed in recognition that not all proposed actions will necessarily have the consequences we think they will have, and that there will probably be unanticipated negative consequences as well. Planning and implementation proceeds then with feedback loops built in, and with an organizational structure and commitment to change actions if needed.

7. Do not compartmentalize management and monitoring—We have experienced several situations where planning has been conducted by technical staff different from the managerial staff that implemented the plan. In a number of cases, planners have left design and implementation of monitoring to managers. This strategy has led to two negative effects: (1) implementing managers have little ownership in and understanding of the rationale for the plan and the actions contained within it, and (2) monitoring becomes viewed as an "add-on" cost for which the organization has no funding. The latter consequence leads to a situation where monitoring is not conducted or is conducted, but the data end up in a box in the ranger station basement without being used for the intended purpose.

Visitor Experience and Resource Protection
Developmental History

The Visitor Experience and Resource Protection (VERP) process was developed by the NPS in the late 1990s (USDI NPS 1997) in response to growing criticisms about its lack of attention to the carrying capacity mandate of the General Authorities Act of 1978. The VERP process was developed to be compatible with the existing General Management Planning process employed by the NPS, and adapted parts of LAC and VIM. Like these two processes, it also employs indicators, standards, and monitoring. It uses the notion of opportunity classes as well.

Visitor Experience and Resource Protection was initially applied in Arches National Park—using a full complement of visitor and biophysical research to identify potential indicators and standards (Manning et al. 1995)—as well as in Acadia National Park (Jacobi and Manning 1999). Following these initial tests, the process was significantly revised and has been used in several national park general management planning processes, including Glacier, Yosemite, and Mount Rainier National Parks. It has undoubtedly been used in other settings as well.

As currently articulated, the application of VERP consists of four major phases involving eight specific elements. These are briefly described below.

Framework Foundation

1. Assemble an interdisciplinary team—For the NPS, assembling an interdisciplinary team to carry out the VERP process (and associated environmental assessments) is a significant step toward embarking on a planning effort. It means that there is recognition that plans must be revised, that significant management issues exist, and that there is a need for coordinated, scientifically informed decisions. Because VERP has been implemented primarily as a component of the NPS General Management Planning process (Freimund et al. 2003, Hof and Lime 1997), designation of staff from both local and service center locations is important to assure technical competency and local staff ownership in the resulting plan.

2. Develop a public involvement strategy—Of all the frameworks discussed here, VERP is the only one that explicitly recognizes the involvement of the public in planning. Although LAC was originally carried out with the involvement of a public-manager-scientist task force, it can be implemented without such involvement. Development of VERP benefited from that experience, and thus a public involvement strategy has become an essential element. Under most circumstances, this would mean that VERP has a high potential to use open, deliberative processes to provide greater opportunities for ownership and implementation (Lachapelle and McCool 2005a)

3. Develop statements of park purpose, significance, and primary interpretive themes; identify planning constraints—This component is designed to develop, communicate, and archive the purposes of the park, the desired futures for it, and the constraints and issues confronting it. This step makes goals, objectives, and values more explicit than in the LAC process, although Cole and McCool (1997) recommended adding a similar step to LAC. By making this step explicit, planners communicate to each other and the public the constraints on management that may exist, identify barriers to achieving goals, and provide direction for what issues need resolution. Essentially, this step produces a "corral" (USDI NPS 1997) identifying and describing the administrative discretion available to respond to management issues (see fig. 9).

Analysis

4. Analyze park resources and existing visitor use—The initial three elements provide the administrative and public engagement foundation needed for planning in addition to determining the overall future direction and conditions for the park in question. In element 4, planners and managers develop an analysis of current conditions, issues, and opportunities faced by the park. These issues and conditions may involve sources of visitor satisfaction and dissatisfaction, areas of visitor use and congestion, transportation facilities and corridors, campgrounds and visitor centers, potential areas of resource sensitivity (such as flood plains, riparian zones, wetlands, and critical habitats), archaeological values, threats to park values, and other conditions that may be problematic and that can be resolved through attention to management of visitors. This analysis may be driven by several factors, including the issues identified by the public, concerns expressed by managers, and the legal mandates governing the park and its administration.

Prescriptions

5. Describe potential range of visitor experience and resource conditions— Following the development of the planning framework and the analysis of park conditions, planners work through a sequence of actions designed to be more prescriptive about the desired future condition of the park. As with LAC, this element recognizes the reality and significance of a diverse range of recreation opportunities and conditions (consistent with park mandates). The sequence of actions in this element involves identifying the potential range of opportunities for park value related visitor experiences—such as wilderness and frontcountry, semideveloped areas, and so on. This step is very similar to the LAC step of developing recreation opportunity classes. The purpose here is to develop descriptions of how the park **could** be managed under various reasonable alternatives. Conceptually, as with LAC, this is the most difficult step, for it involves developing from the abstract, statements about desired future conditions in terms of visitor experiences and related biophysical conditions.

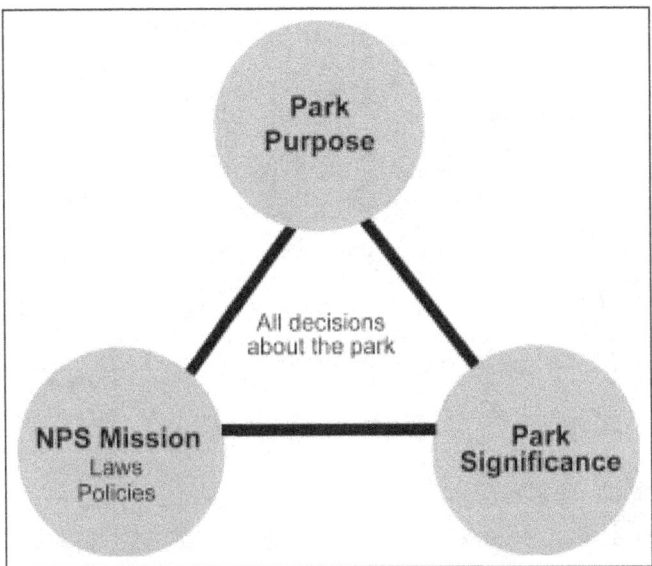

Figure 9—The administrative "corral" describing the limits of discretion to decisionmaking using Visitor Experience and Resource Protection based planning. (Source: USDI National Park Service 1997).

The VERP process, like LAC, breaks down site conditions into three domains:

- Social conditions–the type, amount, and temporal distribution of visitors.

- Biophysical conditions–generally, these descriptions are directed toward the amount of human-induced change in biophysical attributes, not the landscape type.

- Managerial conditions—concerning the amount, type, and visibility of rules, regulations, and managers.

The result of this analysis is a description of the range of conditions within a particular park (see table 7 for an example).

6. Allocate potential zones to specific locations within the park—Element 5 identified the range of recreation opportunities and biophysical and resource conditions that exist within the park. However, the decision to determine what opportunities should exist where is a prescriptive decision, that is, it involves the allocation of park areas to specific zones, and thus identifiable biophysical and social conditions. What factors might be considered in such allocation decisions? One might be influenced by the features, attractions, existing use levels and densities in the park; demand for varying recreation opportunities, the values, mandates,

Table 7—Range of conditions found in Arches National Park following completion of element 5 of Visitor Experience and Resource Protection

Descriptors	Potential management zones								
	Pedestrian	Hiker	Backcountry	Primitive	Motorized sighting	Motorized rural	Semi-primitive motorized	Sensitive resource protection	Developed
Challenge and adventure of experience	Low	Moderate	Moderate-high	Moderate-high	Very low	Low	Moderate	N/a	Very low
Dependence on roads, trails or other facilities	High	Low-moderate	Low	None	Very high	High	Moderate	N/a	Very high
Visitor encounter expectation	Very high	Moderate-high	Low	Very low	Very high	Moderate	Low	N/a	Very high
National Park Service staff encounter expectations	Moderate	Moderate	Low	Very low	Moderate	Low	Very low	N/a	Very high
Identified corridors highest standards–roads	N/a	N/a	N/a	N/a	Paved	Graded dirt	Dirt/rock	N/a	N/a
Identified corridors highest standards–trails	Surfaced, 6 inches wide	Unsurfaced, 2 inches wide	Unsurfaced, 18 inches wide	N/a	Surfaced, 6 inches wide	N/a	N/a	N/a	Surfaced, 6 inches wide
Management action for resource protection and safety	Very high	High	Moderate	Very low	Very high	High	Moderate	Very high	Very high
Tolerance for resource degradation	Low	Low	Very low	Very low	Moderate	Low	Low	None	High

Table 7—Range of conditions found in Arches National Park following completion of element 5 of Visitor Experience and Resource Protection (continued)

	Potential management zones								
Descriptors	**Pedestrian**	**Hiker**	**Backcountry**	**Primitive**	**Motorized sighting**	**Motorized rural**	**Semi-primitive motorized**	**Sensitive resource protection**	**Developed**
Opportunity for solitude	Very low	Low	Moderate	High	Very low	Low	Moderate	N/a	Very low
Noise level	Moderate	Low	Low	Very low	High	Moderate	Moderate	N/a	High
Need for offsite interpretation	High	High	High	High	High	Moderate	Moderate	Very high	High
Appropriateness of onsite interpretation	High	Moderate	Low	Very low	High	Low	Very low	None	High

N/A = not applicable.

Source: USDI National Park Service 1997.

and direction identified and established in element 2 of VERP; public interests; and management concerns. When integrated into environmental analyses, this element allows planners to develop a series of reasonable alternatives, based on various management philosophies (e.g., emphasize primitive recreation, emphasize protecting resources). These alternatives then become the basis for creating understanding of social and environmental consequences.

7. Select indicators and specify standards for each zone; develop a monitoring plan—The VERP process calls for developing indicators (variables measuring identified important social and biophysical conditions), the standards associated with them (the limit of acceptable change), and the appropriate protocols for monitoring them. This element is similar to the LAC process steps 3 and 5 (see previous discussion). In the LAC process, indicators are developed in part to guide what needs to be inventoried, and the standards are developed only following this inventory process.

As VERP has been practiced, the first six elements occur in the GMP process for a specific park.

As VERP has been practiced, the first six elements occur in the GMP process for a specific park. Elements 7 through 9 occur following implementation of the GMP, although they could be incorporated into it. At this time, although many parks have developed prescriptive management zones, few have identified specific indicators, their associated standards, or the protocols for monitoring indicators. This may occur as individual parks come on line for revisions in their GMP and as the need for more quantifiable indicators and associated standards develop.

Monitor and Manage

8. Monitor resource and social indicators—This element involves the periodic and systematic measurement of the indicators identified in element 7 (see USDI NPS 1997 for an extensive discussion of monitoring). The purpose for the monitoring is to understand the effectiveness of management actions implemented to avoid reaching the standards identified in element 7, or to understand effectiveness of management actions in bringing areas back within standard. In this sense, monitoring is an essential component of adaptive management, and processes such as VERP and LAC, when this element is included, can be viewed as adaptive processes. For each indicator identified in element 7, a protocol identifying the spatial and temporal distribution of measurement, the frequency of measurement, and the way in which the monitoring results will be displayed is developed, and eventually implemented.

Monitoring, unfortunately, remains the weakest component of VERP, as well as for other processes such as LAC. As noted earlier, the tendency to separate (compartmentalize) planning and management leads to situations where monitoring is viewed not only as a distinctly separate activity, but one for which few financial resources are available. The VERP and LAC represent attempts to fundamentally change approaches to planning; the extent to which they are not perceived in this way will lead to their ineffective implementation.

9. Take management action—Monitoring alone is inadequate if the resulting data are not evaluated, compared to standards and desired conditions, and needed management action is not taken. The effects of management actions implemented in this element are themselves subject to monitoring and evaluation in order to provide the manager with a continuous loop of information about conditions within the park.

Assessment of Experience With VERP

The VERP and LAC processes are similar frameworks, but not the same. The VERP process was largely derived from the LAC process but adapted to national park situations and the NPS general management planning process. As such, the fundamental premises and concepts are similar to those for LAC, so we do not repeat them here. Because of its more limited application experience, our assessment of experience is brief.

Although VERP has been implemented in several parks as an independent or separate planning process, it has been most generally used as a means of conducting the general management planning process for a park. Where it has been used as a separate process, such as in Arches where it was originally tested, the process has been completed. Where it has been used as a way of conducting a GMP, however, the final set of steps, including identifying standards, is completed after the GMP and associated environmental impact statement have been finalized. This has been usually marked as part of an implementation plan. Unfortunately, few parks have actually identified indicators, their standards, and associated monitoring protocols. Monitoring has yet to occur in any park that has used VERP, although this situation may change. This separation of planning and management has led to the perception that monitoring, for example, is an extra cost and must be funded separately. This condition is not an inherent flaw in VERP but a result of how it is implemented (Hof and Lime 1997). This concerns the organizational will and technical capacity requirements for use of a framework as noted in chapter 3.

Because VERP has been subsumed within the GMP process, it has become more of a way of producing the GMP rather than a separately identifiable process, with some exceptions—such as planning for recreation on the Merced River in Yosemite National Park. This has made use of VERP in other settings more difficult, if only for the lack of good examples from which potential clients can learn about how parks struggled with the nuances of the framework. And unlike LAC, there has been no formal assessment of experience with VERP from which the valuable lessons that planners have learned could be archived. Many other aspects of experience with VERP are similar to what has been learned through application of the LAC process, and readers are referred to that section.

Because VERP emphasizes analysis of resource and social conditions relatively early in the process, there is the chance that data not needed for making decisions may be collected. The VERP process is driven by the "planning corral" (statements of values and park goals), whereas LAC is more driven by issues. These distinctions may lead to significant differences in how the planning is conducted and reflect differing senses of what planning is supposed to do. Finally, VERP explicitly recognizes the role of publics in making park planning decisions by formally recognizing in element 2 the need to develop a public involvement strategy. This recognition is not inherent in the LAC process, although many applications have been informed by the BMWC experience. Element 2 thus provides the foundation for VERP to be open and deliberative.

Because of their similar intellectual lineage, VERP and LAC share similar information requirements, needs for organizational commitment and strengths and weaknesses. Those were articulated in the section describing LAC. Like LAC, VERP can be effective, but that effectiveness is largely a function of organizational will.

Benefits-Based Management
Developmental History

Benefits-based management (BBM) is an approach to recreation planning developed relatively recently that focuses decisionmaking on understanding and managing for certain outcomes of recreational engagements. These outcomes are a result of managerial actions in providing specific attributes of settings, certain visitor-held attributes (such as previous experience, norms, and expectations), and visitor interaction with attributes during a recreational engagement. Initially, the BBM approach rose out of need for increased government accountability in responding to the question of what the public receives for an investment in management of recreation settings. Outcomes of other federal natural resource management programs, such as timber and grazing, had been fairly well known—volume of timber harvested and animal unit months of grazing, for example—but there remains a continuing lack of similar definitive metrics for recreation. Given the lack of metrics, how could recreation management compete for government funding against other services? Borrie and Roggenbuck (1995) argued that a benefits approach helps with "understanding and documentation of the recreation management process and outcomes and by giving the community voice in the planning process."

The BBM is one method of implementing a philosophy generally termed the Benefits Approach to Leisure (BAL) (Driver and Bruns 1999). As these authors argued, the rationale for a BAL was to change the paradigm of recreation management from a focus on inputs (e.g., management actions, such as providing facilities) to the outcomes or results of such inputs (e.g., certain consequences known as benefits) as indicators of what a successful program is. This focus is often described as a change from activity-based management to one focusing on the outputs of management. By focusing on benefits, managers, policymakers, and academics better understand the consequences of decisions which would help in evaluating alternative investments.

The BBM is relatively new, with the earliest formal statements occurring in the mid 1980s (Brown 1984) and early 1990s (Driver et al. 1991a, 1991b; Lee and Driver 1992). These early conceptualizations, however, were developed after a number of years of research on the character of recreational experiences.

Although there has been considerable discussion in the recreation research and applications literature (e.g., Allen 1996, Stein and Lee 1995) concerning BBM, there is currently no definitive, widely accepted document that describes the steps, elements, or processes a planner would follow. The lack of a relatively easy-to-implement and definitive set of steps or processes, we believe is one of the key limiting factors to implementation of BBM.

By focusing on benefits, managers, policymakers, and academics better understand the consequences of decisions which would help in evaluating alternative investments.

Key Concepts

The BAL identifies three types of benefits:

- An improved condition, such as cardiovascular fitness, family cohesiveness, community stability, preserved cultural heritage, stress release, and so on.

- Prevention of a worse condition, such as lost friendships, and prevention of social problems, such as crime.
- Realization of psychological experiences (which accrue only to individuals) such as challenge adventure, skill development, and solitude.

Driver and his associates then use General Systems Theory and the notion of a **recreation production process** to show how inputs and outcomes are related. Basically, this process results from visitors interacting with setting attributes resulting in two stages of outcomes. The first stage results in five types of outcomes:

- Social benefits accruing to communities
- Economic benefits to local communities resulting from managerial investments in recreation settings
- Increased protection to cultural and natural heritage values
- Recreation opportunities
- Any negative consequences

The recreation opportunities produced as a benefit are of three types: activity opportunities, experience opportunities, and other benefit opportunities. In the BAL framework, these initial outcomes of recreational engagements serve as inputs to a secondary "throughput" process that leads to a second-stage set of outcomes. These outcomes involve benefits and costs to individuals and larger groups.

The BBM uses this conceptual structure more specifically to define and configure management of recreational settings. Driver and Bruns suggested that BBM is used in two distinct ways in this context: (1) to optimize an array of benefit opportunities and (2) to use the BAL approach as a basis for intervention to prevent adverse social problems or to capture a specific benefit. For public lands management, the first use is the most common use of BBM, although in communities, the second use may be more dominant.

Although Driver and Bruns argue that BBM can be used for both onsite and offsite customers,[5] our experience suggests that it is most commonly used to implement management for onsite visitors. In this use, managers identify a set of psychological outcomes (experience opportunities in the language of BBM) to be facilitated at a recreation site. This requires not only an assessment of the array of

---

[5] Driver and Bruns prefer to use the term "customer" over visitor or user. Our preference is to use the term visitor because this term implies a perspective we believe to be more appropriate for public land management.

outcomes that could occur, but decisions about what should occur. We, and Driver and associates, specifically use the notion of "facilitate" because visitors produce these outcomes, not managers. Managers can increase the probability of these outcomes occurring, through management of the setting, but cannot ensure that they will occur.

There is a substantial range of psychological outcomes that may occur with any individual recreational engagement. Indeed, Driver and associates (Driver 1992; Driver et al. 1991b, 1996; Lee and Driver 1996; Manfredo et al. 1983) have identified literally dozens. These include learning about and appreciating nature, appreciating scenery, stress release, solitude, being with family or friends, challenge, adventure, humility, independence, freedom, and so on. In any given experience, there may be a "package" of four to six that are dominant. Given this array, a BBM approach to management would select an appropriate package to be facilitated, e.g., freedom, challenge, adventure, solitude, and learning about nature. The managers then would arrange setting attributes to enhance the probability of achieving these outcomes. Satisfactory achievement of these outcomes would then lead to the second-stage benefits mentioned earlier. Management actions to facilitate these outcomes would involve low levels of development, offsite information, and few restrictions on camping and other behaviors.

Pierskalla et al. (2004) studied setting attributes and benefits in nine recreational settings (state parks, ranger districts) in several states. They measured activity participation, setting attributes, and attainment of a variety of benefits. Their study was able to document linkages between attributes and benefit attainment, although the strength of these linkages varied considerably. They also found that for some benefits, activity inputs were more significant than setting inputs, and vice versa. These results suggest that the basic premise of a recreation production process for BBM is more probabilistic than deterministic, a premise similar to initial formulations of ROS by Clark and Stankey (1979).

Knopf et al. (2004) suggested that a BBM approach to planning and management of recreation settings requires six essentials, briefly stated here:

- A shift in paradigm for public land agencies, from being providers of campgrounds, trails, etc. to producing "value-added" changes in individuals and communities.
- A focus on developing explicit management objectives oriented toward identifying specific benefits of public land recreation.
- Linking objectives to specific management prescriptions.

- Development of marketing programs designed to accomplish objectives.
- Implementation of monitoring programs designed to inform planners and managers about how well objectives are being achieved.
- Engagement of all key "service provider" partners (public land recreation providers, private sector business, and host communities).

Assessment of Experience With BBM

The BBM framework represents a significant investment in research (in identifying various psychological outcomes), synthesis (in developing the notion of a recreation production function, and in use of systems theory), and application. In a sense, it views recreational engagements as a rational decisionmaking process by visitors. Once this process is understood, management is then seen as a set of interventions taken to facilitate the positive outcomes of the engagement. The experience with BBM has been limited, however, with reports of its application restricted to one application in an urban area (Borrie and Roggenbuck 1995), and a few cases applied in wildland settings (e.g., Bruns 1998, Stein and Anderson 2002)

Pierskalla et al. (2004) reported on several studies attempting to link recreation setting attributes with benefits. Their results were mixed, with the highest relationships found occurring between activity type and benefit; a few significant relationships occurred between setting conditions and experience. These results suggest that much more work needs to be done to understand the recreation production function, measure site attributes, and establish linkages with expected benefits.

Although some managers have been involved in development and application, the use of BBM as a framework has not spread quickly or widely probably because of the complexity and information requirements needed for its implementation and the lack of a sequence of steps or elements. It seems to us that BBM is more a conceptual approach to how one may think about the purpose and objectives of provision of recreation opportunities on public lands than a practical decisionmaking framework.

Other Frameworks

We mention here two other frameworks that have been used in the past, but have little record of accomplishment. The Tourism Optimization and Management Model (TOMM) was developed in Australia in the 1990s as an approach to managing tourism on Kangeroo Island (Manidis Roberts 1997). The TOMM was derived out of LAC but made public engagement a much more explicit component of the framework (Curtis 2003). Because it focused on managing tourism, the name was changed to not only include that word, but to eliminate the word "limits" so the framework would appeal to the tourism industry. In addition, the notions of indicators and standards are not as explicit in TOMM as they are in LAC. Although TOMM is often reviewed in the literature assessing various frameworks, it has not received widespread application.

Using similar notions of objective-based management, indicators, and standards, Visitor Impact Management (VIM) was developed to respond to the mandate in the General Authorities Act of 1978 (for the NPS) to identify carrying capacities (Graefe et al. 1990). The process was tested and applied in a variety of settings but was never really adopted by the NPS as a planning framework. This was probably a result of a substantial lack of collaboration in its development, ownership by NPS in the framework, and its site-level orientation.

The VIM, like the VERP and LAC, contains a number of steps focused around standards, indicators, and objectives. Although VIM has several similarities to LAC, and was developed contemporaneously with it, it is not the same. The VIM does not explicitly include the notion of opportunity classes and focuses primarily on very small sites—such as a viewpoint—whereas VERP and LAC are much broader in their orientation and application. Both processes use indicators and standards and argue for including monitoring as a fundamental, inherent task of management.

Chapter 5: Conclusions

Public land recreation managers have several frameworks to choose from to assist in addressing the growing diversity and complexity of recreation and tourism development issues. The Recreation Opportunity Spectrum (ROS), Limits of Acceptable Change LAC), and Visitor Experience and Resource Protection (VERP) frameworks have the advantage of empirical research and managerial experience (although more limited for VERP) to guide their application, determine construct validity, and in considering questions of appropriateness. Benefits-Based Management (BBM) is an approach that has driven a considerable amount of thought but few complete applications in terms of a formally defined framework process. Similar to BBM, recreation and tourism carrying capacity has been responsible for a tremendous amount of research into the relationship between use levels and biophysical and social conditions. The practical utility of this approach, however, is extremely limited by an unproven empirical foundation, lack of process, and reductionistic tendencies.

The development of recreation and tourism frameworks has been more evolutionary than revolutionary.

The development of recreation and tourism frameworks has been more evolutionary than revolutionary. For example, the ROS evolved out of a number of concept papers recognizing that visitors to public lands sought a variety of settings. Although it took some time, ROS eventually evolved into a formalized planning process that could be integrated into planning for public lands. The popularity of ROS led it to be applied to similar issues and resulted in frameworks, such as the Tourism Opportunity Spectrum and the Water Recreation Opportunity Spectrum. Although many of the evolving adaptations represent new insights and a level of creativity in how a concept can be applied in different situations, the ROS, as a concept, remains at the core of the planning frameworks identified here.

The LAC and VERP adapted ROS to formally designated public land recreation settings (such as wilderness and national parks) and extended it to include indicators, standards, and monitoring. All three processes are based on the premise of a demand hierarchy, that is, people engage in activities within certain settings to achieve particular outcomes. Successful attainment of these outcomes leads to certain benefits. The BBM is also premised on the demand hierarchy, but focuses on identifying the benefits first, then manipulating setting characteristics to achieve those benefits. Although LAC and VERP were initially developed for formally designated areas, they can be and have been applied in other settings as well.

There have been other assessments conducted of recreation planning frameworks (e.g., Manning 2004, Moore et al. 2003, Nilsen and Tayler 1997). These assessments, however, have been more descriptive than evaluative, focusing primarily on the **characteristics** of the frameworks rather than on their **performance** (e.g., if they contain indicators). Their **suitability** for addressing issues confronting public land decisionmakers or their **experience** in specific situations have generally not been addressed in the literature. Of the frameworks discussed here, only LAC has had a formal evaluation involving scientists and managers that has appeared in the literature (McCool and Cole 1997a).

Evaluation is important. This is a fundamental way in which we learn. Evaluation helps us address questions important in any management environment: Are management actions effective? How do frameworks help managers make decisions? How can experience be used systematically to inform actions and frameworks? Such questions are essential to improving an agency's technical ability to respond to new issues as well as old ones. Unfortunately, monitoring performance and evaluating experience are rarely conducted in public land recreation and tourism development decisions. For example, McCool (2001) indicated that the efficacy of recreation use limit policies, in spite of their relatively frequent use, has never been formally evaluated and reported. Institutions may not be particularly well designed for current and future challenges (Stankey et al. 2003b).

Successful framework applications have occurred, in our judgment, as a result of close, continuing collaboration of managers and scientists. As we noted earlier, such collaboration allows managers to communicate issues and mandates clearer to scientists, scientists can query managers and come to a better understanding of the job at hand, and as a result develop applications, concepts, and processes that are more useful to managers. Approaches to recreation and tourism development issues that have not involved this collaboration (frequently found in refereed journal articles), in general, have not had widespread application.

If a framework can be viewed as an innovation, then adoption of this innovation follows a certain and generally predictable path (Rogers 1995). Rogers argued that the adoption of an innovation by a member of a social system (say a manager) depends heavily on the decisions of other members of the social (managerial) system. We expand this to include the experience of other members of the system with the particular innovation. The close collaboration of scientists and managers that typified the development of the ROS, LAC, VERP, and BBM frameworks allowed managers to adopt the innovation in small steps, and with the support of scientists.

Positive experiences of other members of the social system (in Rogers' language, innovators and early adopters) provide the confirmation that the innovation will enhance a person's ability to function effectively. Such experiences reduce the

Successful framework applications have occurred, in our judgment, as a result of close, continuing collaboration of managers and scientists.

risk of adopting an innovation that may fail. This process certainly occurred with the LAC system following its use in the Bob Marshall Wilderness in the mid 1980s. Other managers, once they heard of the use of LAC there, frequently called and asked for information, why the process was successful, and for help in adopting it for their own areas.

Not all innovations diffuse at the same rate or are adopted at the same time. There are always late adopters and laggards (in Rogers' terms). Agencies attempt to deal with this by codifying and putting in agency manuals and handbooks the innovative frameworks (this was done with ROS and VERP, but not LAC[1] or BBM). Although there may be a good rationale for doing this, adoption in a specific situation is more a function of a manager's willingness to assume certain risks to gain certain benefits (will it work, will the framework save me time, will it solve problems), which in turn is a function of a number of personal variables.

The ROS was a valuable innovation, not because of its codification, but because it helped managers understand and integrate recreation into decisions in a multiple-use situation. The LAC succeeded, in our judgment, because it helped managers structure their thinking about the tradeoffs between partially conflicting goals. The VERP is not working as well, not because of any structural flaws in its design, but because of how it has been applied in general management planning. The BBM, as a decisionmaking framework, has not been widely adopted, despite concerted efforts, probably because it is often portrayed as very complex. If managers do not understand an innovation, it is unlikely they will adopt it. However, BBM has stimulated a great deal of empirical research and activity around the notion of the products of public land recreation.

Innovations and bureaucracies are polar opposites. Bureaucracies, such as land management agencies, are established to deal with routine problems and issues. Land management agencies are notoriously conservative, with a top-down command and control structure. In these situations, innovations are slow to come. Diffusion strategies must emphasize, Rogers argues, the compatibility of the innovation with existing agency norms and policies. Visitor Impact Management (VIM) for example, was not extensively applied in the National Park System (NPS), the agency for which it was designed. It was not until NPS planners saw the ability to integrate VIM and LAC with the agency's existing general management planning

---

[1] The LAC process was initially published as a Forest Service General Technical Report, but it is not formalized in the Forest Service Manual.

process that the ideas of these frameworks were actually applied and tested as the VERP system. Incidentally, VIM itself was not developed collaboratively, but the VERP process involved much collaborative development between managers and scientists.

Given the complex, contentious, and changing environment in which recreation and tourism development decisions are being made, there is a need to continually understand the strengths and weaknesses of these frameworks, to monitor the situations in which they work or do not work, and to periodically make changes in their implementation. Use of approaches such as recreation carrying capacity not only miscasts a particular issue, but wastes scarce planning resources when managers confront the unresolved issue time after time. The limited capacity of public land agencies to manage recreation inevitably leads to the conclusion that decision-makers must have a better understanding of these frameworks, the key concepts and assumptions upon which they are built, and their suitability for addressing different issues. Developing capacity in these areas ultimately will lead to more efficient, effective, and equitable decisions.

In all this discussion, it is important to keep in mind the conceptual validity of the framework. The conceptual foundations for approaches such as carrying capacity are contested in the scientific literature. They remain more hypotheses about relationships than functional concepts and frameworks useful for structuring deliberation. Despite their appealing simplicity, they have been difficult to implement in such a way that they make for easy adoption. The ROS, LAC, VERP, and BBM are built on a deliberative model of science—iterative cycles of inductive and deductive reasoning, hypothesis testing, and real world application.

Acknowledgments

This research is part of the Recreation and Tourism Initiative. Funding came through the Focused Science Delivery Program and the Human and Natural Resource Interactions Program of the Pacific Northwest Research Station. The authors acknowledge and appreciate comments and assistance by Kelly Lawrence, Lee Cerveny, and Linda Kruger of the Pacific Northwest Research Station; Bob Dvorak and John Adams, graduate students at The University of Montana; Perry Brown, Dean of the College of Forestry and Conservation, The University of Montana; and R. Neil Moisey, a faculty member at The University of Montana. The authors also appreciate the helpful comments of the three peer reviewers.

References

Allen, G.M.; Gould, E.M., Jr. 1986. Complexity, wickedness, and public forests. Journal of Forestry. 84(4): 20–23.

Allen, L. 1996. A primer: benefits-based management of recreation services. Parks and Recreation. March: 64–76.

Arnstein, S.R. 1969. A ladder of citizen participation. Journal of the American Institute of Planners. 35(7): 216–224.

Ashor, J.L.; McCool, S. 1984. Politics and rivers: creating effective citizen involvement in management decisions in proceedings, national river recreation symposium. Baton Rouge, LA: Louisiana State University: 136–151.

Beale, C.L.; Johnson, K.M. 1998. The identification of recreational counties in nonmetropolitan areas of the USA. Population Research and Policy Review. 17: 37–53.

Borrie, W.T.; McCool, S.F.; Stankey, G.H. 1998. Protected area planning principles and strategies. In: Lindberg, K.; Wood, M.E.; Engeldrum, D., eds. Ecotourism: a guide for planners and managers. North Bennington, VT: The Ecotourism Society: 133–154. Vol. 2.

Borrie, W.T.; Roggenbuck, J.W. 1995. Community-based research of an urban recreation application of benefits-based management. In: Chavez, D.J., tech. coord. Proceedings, second symposium on social aspects of recreation research. Gen. Tech. Rep. PSW-156. Riverside, CA: U.S. Department of Agriculture, Forest Service, Pacific Southwest Research Station: 159–163.

Boyd, S.W.; Butler, R.W. 1996. Managing ecotourism: an opportunity spectrum approach. Tourism Management. 17(8): 557–566.

Brewer, G.D. 1973. Politicians, bureaucrats, and the consultant: a critique of urban problem solving. New York: Basic Books. 291 p.

British Columbia Ministry of Forests. 1991. Recreation manual. http://www.for.gov.bc.ca/hfp/rec/manual/index.htm. (September 8, 2005).

British Columbia Ministry of Forests. 1998. Recreation Opportunity Spectrum inventory: procedures and standards manual. Vancouver, BC: Forest Practices Branch for Resources Inventory Committee. Version 3.0.

Brown, K.; Turner, R.K.; Hameed, H.; Bateman, I. 1997. Environmental carrying capacity and tourism development in the Maldives and Nepal. Environmental Conservation. 24: 316–325.

Brown, P.J. 1984. Benefits of outdoor recreation and some ideas for valuing recreation opportunities. In: Peterson, G.L.; Randal, A., eds. Valuation of wildland recreation benefits. Boulder, CO: Westview Press: 209–220.

Brown, P.J.; Driver, B.L.; McConnell, C. 1978. The opportunity spectrum concept and behavioral information in outdoor recreation resource supply inventories: background and application. In: Lund, G.H.; LaBau, V.J.; Ffolliott, P.F.; Robinson, D.W., tech. cords. Integrated inventories of renewable natural resources: proceedings of the workshop. Gen. Tech. Rep. RM-55. Fort Collins, CO: U.S. Department of Agriculture, Forest Service, Rocky Mountain Forest and Range Experiment Station: 73–84.

Bruns, D. 1998. Personal communication. State Recreation program leader, USDI Bureau of Land Management, 2850 Youngfield Street, Lakewood, CO 80215.

Butler, R.W.; Waldbrook, L.A. 1991. A new planning tool: the tourism opportunity spectrum. Journal of Tourism Studies. 2(1): 4–14.

Carey, D.I. 1993. Development based on carrying capacity: a strategy for environmental protection. Global Environmental Change. 3: 140–148.

Carroll, M.S.; Blatner, K.A. 1994. Forest-based communities in the "Blues:" adapting to environmental and social change. Tech. Note. BMNRI-TN-3. La Grande, OR: Blue Mountains Natural Resources Institute.

Cessford, G. 1995. Off-road mountain biking: a profile of participants and their recreation setting and experience preferences. New Zealand: Department of Conservation. http://www.mountainbike.co.nz/politics/doc/profile/index.htm. (June 30, 2006).

Clark, R.N. 1982. Promises and pitfalls of the ROS in resource management. Australian Parks and Recreation. May: 9–13.

Clark, R.N.; Stankey, G. 1979. The recreation opportunity spectrum: a framework for planning, management and research. Gen. Tech. Rep. PNW-GTR-98. Portland, OR: U.S. Department of Agriculture, Forest Service, Pacific Northwest Forest and Range Experiment Station. 32 p.

Cole, D.N. 1995. Recreational trampling experiments: effects of trampler weight and shoe type. Res. Note INT-RN-425. Ogden, UT: U.S. Department of Agriculture, Forest Service, Intermountain Research Station. 4 p.

Cole, D.N.; McCool, S.F. 1997. Limits of acceptable change and natural resources planning: When is LAC useful, when is it not? In: McCool, S.F.; Cole, D.N., comps. Proceedings—limits of acceptable change and related planning processes: progress and future directions. Gen. Tech. Rep. INT-GTR-371. Ogden, UT: U.S. Department of Agriculture, Forest Service, Rocky Mountain Research Station: 69–71.

Cole, D.N.; Stankey, G.H. 1997. Historical development of limits of acceptable change: conceptual clarifications and possible extensions. In: McCool, S.F.; Cole, D.N., comps. Proceedings—limits of acceptable change and related planning processes: progress and future directions. Gen. Tech. Rep. INT-GTR-371. Ogden, UT: U.S. Department of Agriculture, Forest Service, Rocky Mountain Research Station: 5–9.

Convention on Biological Diversity. 2005. Biological diversity and tourism. http://www.biodiv.org/programmes/socio-eco/tourism/guidelines.asp?page=6. (June 30, 2006).

Cooney, R.; Dickson, B. 2005. Biodiversity and the precautionary principle: risk and uncertainty in conservation and sustainable use. London: EarthScan. 272 p.

Curtis, N. 2003. Managing commercial recreation on Crown land in British Columbia: a policy evaluation. Vancouver, BC: Simon Fraser University. Pgs. M.S. thesis.

Dana, S.T. 1957. Problem analysis: research in forest recreation. Washington, DC: U.S. Department of Agriculture, Forest Service. 36 p.

Dawson, C.P. 2001. Ecotourism and nature-based tourism: one end of the tourism opportunity spectrum? In: McCool, S.F.; Moisey, R.N., eds. Tourism, recreation and sustainability: linking culture and the environment. New York: CABI Publishing: 41–53.

Driver, B. 1992. The benefits of leisure. Parks and Recreation. 27(11): 16–25.

Driver, B.; Brown, P.J.; Stankey, G.H.; Gregoire, T.G. 1987. The ROS planning system: evolution, basic concepts, and research needed. Leisure Sciences. 9(2): 201–212.

Driver, B.L.; Brown, P.J. 1978. The opportunity spectrum concept and behavior information in outdoor recreation resource supply inventories. In: Lund, G.H.; LaBau, V.J.; Ffolliott, P.F.; Robinson, D.W., tech. cords. Integrated inventories of renewable natural resources: proceedings of the workshop. Gen. Tech. Rep. RM-55. Fort Collins, CO: U.S. Department of Agriculture, Forest Service, Rocky Mountain Forest and Range Experiment Station: 24–31.

Driver, B.L.; Brown, P.J.; Peterson, G.L., eds. 1991a. Benefits of leisure. State College, PA: Venture Publishing, Inc. 483 p.

Driver, B.L.; Bruns, D.H. 1999. Concepts and uses of the benefits approach to leisure. In: Jackson, E.L.; Burton, T.L., eds. Leisure studies: prospects for the twenty-first century. State College, PA: Venture Publishing, Inc.: 349–369.

Driver, B.L.; Dustin, D.; Baltic, T.; Elsner, G.; Peterson, G., eds. 1996. Nature, spirit and landscape management. Nature and human spirit: toward an expanded land management ethic. State College, PA: Venture Publishing, Inc. 497 p.

Driver, B.L.; Tinsley, H.E.A.; Manfredo, M.J. 1991b. The paragraphs about leisure and recreation experience preference scales: results of two inventories designed to assess the breadth of the perceived psychological benefits. In: Driver, B.L.; Brown, P.J.; Peterson, G.L., eds. Benefits of leisure. State College, PA: Venture Publishing, Inc.: 263–286.

Drucker, P.F. 1986. The changed world economy. Foreign Affairs. 64(4): 768–791.

Faludi, A. 1973. Planning theory. Oxford, United Kingdom: Pergamon Press. 306 p.

Farrell, T.A.; Marion, J.L. 2002. The protected area visitor impact management (PAVIM) framework: a simplified process for making management decisions. Journal of Sustainable Tourism. 10(1): 31–51.

Federal Advisory Committee Act. [FACA]. 1972. Act of October 6, 1972. Stat. 77. 5 U.S.C. Appendix 2.

Federal Land Policy and Management Act. [FLPMA]. 1976. Act of October 21, 1976. 43 U.S.C. 1701(note).

Fortmann, L.; Kusel, J. 1991. New voices, old beliefs: forest environmental values among new and long-standing rural residents. Rural Sociology. 55(2): 214–232.

Friedmann, J. 1973. Retracking America. New York: Anchor/Doubleday. 289 p.

Friedmann, J. 1987. Planning in the public domain: from knowledge to action. Princeton, NJ: Princeton University Press. 501 p.

Freimund, W.; Peel, S.; Bradybaugh, J.; Manning, R.E. 2003. The wilderness experience as purported by planning compared with that of visitors to Zion National Park. In: Proceedings, George Wright Society annual conference. Hancock, MI: George Wright Society: 276–280.

Frissell, S.S., Jr.; Stankey, G.H. 1972. Wilderness environmental quality: the search for social and ecological harmony. In: Proceedings, Society of American Foresters annual conference. Washington, DC: Society of American Foresters: 170–183.

General Authorities Act. 1978. 84 Stat. 825.

Graber, E.F. 1974. Newcomers and oldtimers: growth and change in a mountain town. Rural Sociology. 39(4): 504–513.

Graefe, A.R.; Kuss, F.R.; Vaske, J.J. 1990. Visitor impact management: a planning framework. Washington, DC: National Parks and Conservation Association. 105 p.

Haas, G.E. 2002. Visitor capacity on public lands and waters: making better decisions. Ashburn, VA: National Parks and Recreation Association. 42 p. A report of the Federal Interagency Task Force on visitor capacity on public lands. Submitted to the Assistant Secretary for Fish and Wildlife and Parks, U.S. Department of the Interior, Washington, DC 20240.

Haas, G.E. 2004. On the water front—vital judicial ruling addresses visitor capacity. Parks and Recreation. 39(9): 106–113.

Haas, G.; Aukerman, R.; Lovejoy, V.; Welch, D. 2004. Water Recreation Opportunity Spectrum (WROS) users' guidebook. Denver, CO: U.S. Department of the Interior, Bureau of Reclamation. 95 p.

Hamill, L. 1984. River recreation resource inventory and the ROS method. In: National river recreation symposium. Baton Rouge, LA: Louisiana State University School of Landscape Architecture: 507–522.

He,W.; Sengupta, M.; Velkoff, V.A.; DeBarros, K.A. 2005. 65+ in the United States. In: Current population reports series. Washington, DC: Government Printing Office: 23–209.

Hof, M.; Lime, D.W. 1997. Visitor experience and resource protection framework in the National Park System: rationale, current status, and future direction. In: McCool, S.F.; Cole, D.N., comps. Proceedings—limits of acceptable change and related planning processes: progress and future directions. Gen. Tech. Rep. INT-GTR-371. Ogden, UT: U.S. Department of Agriculture, Forest Service, Rocky Mountain Research Station: 29–36.

Jacobi, C.; Manning, R. 1999. Crowding and conflict on the carriage roads of Acadia National Park: an application of the visitor experience and resource protection framework. Park Science. 19(2): 22–26.

Jasanoff, S. 1990. The fifth branch: science advisers and policymakers. Cambridge, MA: Harvard University Press. 302 p.

Knopf, R.C.; Andereck, K.L.; Tucker, K.; Bottomly, B.; Virdent, R.J. 2004. Building connections among lands, people and communities: a case study of benefits-based management plan development for the Gunnison Gorge National Conservation Area. In: Proceedings, fourth social aspects and recreation research symposium. San Francisco, CA: San Francisco State University, Department of Recreation and Leisure Studies: 170–179.

Kruger, L.E.; Jakes, P.J. 2003. The importance of place: advances in science and application. Forest Science. 49(6): 819–821.

Krumpe, E.; McCool, S.F. 1997. Role of public involvement in the limits of acceptable change wilderness planning system. In: McCool, S.F.; Cole, D.N., comps. Proceedings—limits of acceptable change and related planning processes: progress and future directions. Gen. Tech. Rep. INT-GTR-371. Ogden, UT: U.S. Department of Agriculture, Forest Service, Rocky Mountain Research Station: 16–20.

Lachapelle, P.; McCool, S.F. 2005a. Exploring the concept of "ownership" in natural resource planning. Society and Natural Resources. 18: 279–285.

Lachapelle, P.; McCool, S.F. 2005b. Visitor experience indicators: a workshop for eastern Arctic Canadian National Parks. Missoula, MT: College of Forestry and Conservation, The University of Montana. 45 p.

Lake Ripley Management District. 2003. Lake Ripley watercraft census and recreational carrying capacity analysis. Cambridge WI: Lake Ripley Management District.

Lee, M.; Driver, B. 1996. Benefits-based management: a new paradigm for managing amenity resources. In: Burch, W., Jr.; Aley, J.; Conover, B.; Field, D., eds. Survival of the organizationally fit: ecosystem management as an adaptive strategy for natural resource organizations in the 21st century. New York: Taylor and Francis Publishers: 143–154.

Leung, Y.; Marion, J.L. 2000. Recreation impacts and management in wilderness: a state-of-knowledge review. In: Cole, D.N.; McCool, S.; Borrie, W.T.; O'Loughlin, J., eds. Proceedings, wilderness science in a time of change conference: wilderness ecosystems, threats and management. RMRS-P-15-VOL-5. Ogden, UT: U.S. Department of Agriculture, Forest Service, Rocky Mountain Research Station: 23–48. Vol. 5.

Lime, D.W. 1970. Research for determining use capacities of the Boundary Waters Canoe Area. Naturalist. 21(4): 9–13.

Lime, D.W.; Stankey, G.H. 1971. Carrying capacity: maintaining outdoor recreation quality. In: Larson, E.H., ed. Recreation symposium proceedings. Upper Darby, PA: U.S. Department of Agriculture, Forest Service, Northeastern Forest Experiment Station: 174–184.

Lucas, R.C. 1964. The recreational capacity of the Quetico-Superior area. St. Paul, MN: U.S. Department of Agriculture, Lake States Forest and Experiment Station. 34 p.

Lucas, R.C. 1985. Visitor characteristics, attitudes and use patterns in the Bob Marshall Wilderness Complex. Res. Pap. INT-345. Ogden, UT: U.S. Department of Agriculture, Forest Service, Intermountain Research Station. 32 p.

Manfredo, M.J.; Driver, B.; Brown, P.J. 1983. A test of concepts inherent in experience based setting management for outdoor recreation areas. Journal of Leisure Research. 15(3): 262–283.

Manidis Roberts. 1997. Developing a tourism optimization management model (TOMM), a model to monitor and manage tourism on Kangaroo Island, South Australia. Surry Hills, New South Wales: Manidis Roberts Consultants.

Manning, R.; Lime, D.; Hof, M.; Freimund, W. 1995. The visitor experience and resource protection (VERP) process: the application of carrying capacity to Arches National Park. The George Wright Forum. 12(3): 41–55.

Manning, R.; Valliere, W.; Menteer, B. 1999. Values, ethics and attitudes toward national forest management: an empirical study. Society and Natural Resources. 12 (5): 421–436.

Manning, R.E. 2004. Recreation planning frameworks. Society and natural resources: a summary of knowledge. Jefferson, MO: Modern Litho: 83–96.

McCool, S.F. 1989. Limits of acceptable change: some principles towards serving visitors and managing our resources. In: Graham, R.; Lawrence, R., eds. Proceedings of a North American workshop on visitor management in parks and protected areas. Waterloo, ON: University of Waterloo: 194–200.

McCool, S.F. 2001. Limiting recreational use in wilderness: research issues and management challenges in appraising their effectiveness. In: Freimund, W.A.; Cole, D.N., comps. Proceedings. RMRS-P-20. Ogden, UT: U.S. Department of Agriculture, Forest Service, Rocky Mountain Research Station: 49–55.

McCool, S.F.; Ashor, J.L.; Stokes, G.L. 1985. An alternative to rational-comprehensive planning: transactive planning. In: Lucas, R.C., comp. Proceedings—national wilderness research conference: current research. Gen. Tech. Rep. INT-212. Ogden, UT: U.S. Department of Agriculture, Forest Service, Rocky Mountain Research Station.

McCool, S.F.; Cole, D.N. 1997a. Experiencing limits of acceptable change: some thoughts after a decade of implementation. In: McCool, S.F.; Cole, D.N., comps. Proceedings—limits of acceptable change and related planning processes: progress and future directions. Gen. Tech. Rep. INT-GTR-371. Ogden, UT: U.S. Department of Agriculture, Forest Service, Rocky Mountain Research Station: 72–78.

McCool, S.F.; Cole, D.N., comps. 1997b. Proceedings—limits of acceptable change and related planning processes: progress and future directions. Gen. Tech. Rep. INT-GTR-371. Ogden, UT: U.S. Department of Agriculture, Forest Service, Rocky Mountain Research Station. 84 p.

McCool, S.F.; Cole, D.N. 2001. Thinking and acting regionally: toward better decisions about appropriate conditions, standards and restrictions on recreation use. George Wright Forum. 18(3): 85–98.

McCool, S.F.; Guthrie, K.; Smith, J.K. 2000. Building consensus: Legitimate hope or seductive paradox? Res. Pap. RP-25. Fort Collins, CO: U.S. Department of Agriculture, Forest Service, Rocky Mountain Research Station. 14 p.

McCool, S.F.; Kruger, L.E. 2003. Human migration and natural resources: implications for land managers and challenges for researchers. Gen. Tech. Rep. PNW-GTR-580. Portland, OR: U.S. Department of Agriculture, Forest Service, Pacific Northwest Research Station. 18 p.

McCool, S.F.; Lime, D.W. 2001. Tourism carrying capacity: Tempting fantasy or useful reality? Journal of Sustainable Tourism. 9(5): 372–388.

McCool, S.F.; Stankey, G. 1991. Recreation use limits: the wildlife manager's continuing dilemma. Western Wildlands. 16(4): 2–7.

McCoy, K.L.; Krumpe, E.; Allen, S. 1995. Limits of acceptable change planning-evaluation implementation by the U.S. Forest Service. International Journal of Wilderness. 1(2): 18–22.

McGranahan, D.A. 1999. Natural amenities drive rural population change. Agric. Econ. Rep. 781. Washington, DC: U.S. Department of Agriculture, Food and Rural Economics Division, Economic Research Service. 24 p.

Moore, S.A.; Smith, A.J.; Newsome, D.N. 2003. Environmental performance reporting for natural area tourism: contributions by visitor impact management frameworks and their indicators. Journal of Sustainable Tourism. 11(4): 348–375.

More, T.A.; Bulmer, S.; Henzel, L.; Mates, A.E. 2003. Extending the recreation opportunity spectrum to nonfederal lands in the Northeast: an implementation guide. Gen. Tech. Rep. GTR-NE-309. Newtown Square, PA: U.S. Department of Agriculture, Forest Service, Northeastern Research Station. 25 p.

Multiple Use Sustained Yield Act of 1960 [MUSYA]; Act of June 12, 1960, 16 U.S.C. (note), 528–531.

National Environmental Policy Act of 1969 [NEPA]; 42 U.S.C. 4321 et seq.

National Forest Management Act of 1976 [NFMA]; Act of October 22, 1976; 16 U.S.C. 1600.

Newsome, D.N.; Moore, S.A.; Dowling, R.K. 2002. Natural area tourism: ecology, impacts and management. Buffalo, NY: Channel View Publications. 340 p.

Nilsen, P.; Tayler, G. 1997. A comparative analysis of protected area planning and management frameworks. In: McCool, S.F.; Cole, D.N., comps. Proceedings— limits of acceptable change and related planning processes: progress and future directions. Gen. Tech. Rep. INT-GTR-371. Ogden, UT: U.S. Department of Agriculture, Forest Service, Rocky Mountain Research Station: 49–57.

Osborne, D.E.; Gaebler, T. 1992. Reinventing government: how the entrepreneurial spirit is transforming the public sector. Reading, MA: Addison-Wesley Publishing Co. 432 p.

O'Toole, R. 1988. Reforming the Forest Service. Washington, DC: Island Press. 247 p.

Patterson, M.; Watson, A.; Roggenbuck, J.W. 1998. An hermeneutic approach to studying the nature of wilderness experiences. Journal of Leisure Research. 30(4): 423–452.

Pierskalla, C.D.; Lee, M.A.; Stein, T.V.; Anderson, D.H.; Nickerson, R. 2004. Understanding relationships among recreation opportunities: a meta-analysis of nine studies. Leisure Sciences. 26: 163–180.

Rischbieter, D. 2004. Recreation carrying capacity: Oroville facilities relicensing. FERC Project No. 2100. Sacramento, CA: State of California, Department of Water Resources.

Robson, M.; Eagles, P.F.J. 2002. Hiking opportunity spectrum: landscape and facility preferences of wilderness hikers in Ontario, Canada. Journal of Tourism. 5(1): 67–76.

Roe, E.M. 1997. On rangeland carrying capacity. Journal of Range Management. 50: 467–472.

Rogers, E.M. 1995. Diffusion of innovation. New York: The Free Press, Simon and Schuster. 512 p.

Rudzitis, G.; Johansen, H.E. 1989. Migration into western wilderness counties: causes and consequences. Western Wildlands. Spring: 19–23.

Saveriades, A. 2000. Establishing the social carrying capacity for tourist resorts of the east coast of the Republic of Cyprus. Tourism Management. 21(2): 147–156.

Schomaker, J. 1984. Writing quantifiable river recreation management objectives. In: Popadic, J.S.; Butterfield, D.I.; Anderson, D.H.; Popadic, M.R., eds. Proceedings, national river recreation management symposium. Baton Rouge, LA: Louisiana State University: 249–253.

Seidl, I.; Tisdell, C.A. 1999. Carrying capacity reconsidered: from Malthus' population theory to cultural carrying capacity. Ecological Economics. 31: 395–408.

Shafer, E.L. 1969. The average camper who doesn't exist. Res. Pap. NE-142. Upper Darby, PA: U.S. Department of Agriculture, Forest Service, Northeastern Forest Experiment Station. 27 p.

Shelby, B.; Heberlein, T. 1986. Carrying capacity in recreation settings. Corvallis, OR: Oregon State University Press. 164 p.

Stankey, G.H. 1972. A strategy for the definition and management of wilderness quality. In: Krutilla, J., ed. Natural environments: studies in theoretical and applied analysis. Baltimore, MD; London: Johns Hopkins University Press: 88–114.

Stankey, G.H. 1973. Visitor perception of wilderness recreation carrying capacity. Res. Pap. INT-142. Ogden, UT: U.S. Department of Agriculture, Forest Service, Intermountain Forest and Range Experiment Station. 61 p.

Stankey, G.H. 1999. The recreation opportunity spectrum and the limits of acceptable change planning systems: a review of experiences and lessons in ecosystem management. In: Aley, J.; Burch, W.R., Jr.; Conover, B.; Field, D., eds. Adaptive strategies for natural resources organizations in the twenty-first century Philadelphia, PA: Taylor and Francis: 173–188.

Stankey, G.H.; Baden, J. 1977. Rationing wilderness use: methods, problems, and guidelines. Res. Pap. INT-192. Ogden, UT: U.S. Department of Agriculture, Forest Service, Intermountain Research Station. 20 p.

Stankey, G.H.; Bormann, B.T.; Ryan, C.; Shindler, B.; Sturtevant, V.; Clark, R.N.; Philpot, C. 2003a. Adaptive management and the Northwest Forest Plan: rhetoric and reality. Journal of Forestry. 101: 40–46.

Stankey, G.H.; Brown, P.J.; Clark, R.N. 1983. Monitoring and evaluating changes and trends in recreation opportunity supply. In: Bell, J.F.; Atterbury, T., eds. Renewable resource inventories for monitoring changes and trends: proceedings of an international conference. Corvallis, OR: College of Forestry, Oregon State University: 227–230.

Stankey, G.H.; Clark, R.N. 1996. Frameworks for decision making in management. In: Miller, M., ed. Proceedings of the 1996 world congress on coastal and marine tourism. Seattle, WA: University of Washington; Eugene, OR: University of Oregon: 55–59.

Stankey, G.H.; Cole, D.N.; Lucas, R.C.; Petersen, M.E.; Frissell, S.S. 1985. The limits of acceptable change (LAC) system for wilderness planning. Gen. Tech. Rep. INT-176. Ogden, UT: U.S. Department of Agriculture, Forest Service, Intermountain Research Station. 37 p.

Stankey, G.H.; McCool, S.F. 1984. Carrying capacity in recreational settings: evolution, appraisal and application. Leisure Sciences. 6(4): 453–473.

Stankey, G.H.; McCool, S.F. 1991. Recreation use limits: the wildland manager's continuing dilemma. Western Wildlands. 17(Winter): 2–7.

Stankey, G.H.; McCool, S.F.; Clark, R.N. 2003b. Building innovative institutions for ecosystem management: integrating analysis and inspiration. In: Shindler, B.A.; Beckley, T.M.; Finley, M.C., eds. Two paths toward sustainable forests: public values in Canada and the United States. Corvallis, OR: Oregon State University Press: 271-295.

Stankey, G.H.; McCool, S.F.; Stokes, G.L. 1984. Limits of acceptable change: a new framework for managing the Bob Marshall Wilderness Complex. Western Wildlands. 10(3): 33–37.

Steel, B.; List, P.; Shindler, B. 1994. Conflicting values about federal forests: a comparison of national and Oregon publics. Society Natural Resources: 137–153.

Steel, B.; Weber, E. 2003. Ecosystem management and public opinion in the United States. In: Shindler, B.A.; Beckley, T.M.; Finley, M.C., eds. Two paths toward sustainable forests: public values in Canada and the United States. Corvallis, OR: Oregon State University Press: 76–92.

Stein, T.V.; Anderson, D.H. 2002. Combining benefits-based management with ecosystem management for landscape planning: Leech Lake watershed, Minnesota. Landscape and Urban Planning. 60(3): 151–161.

Stein, T.; Lee, M.E. 1995. Managing recreation resources for positive outcomes: an application of benefits-based management. Journal of Park and Recreation Administration. 13(3): 52–70.

Stokes, G.L. 1990. The evolution of wilderness management. Journal of Forestry. 88(10): 15–20.

Stokols, D. 1972. On the distinction between density and crowding: some implications for future research. Psychological Review. 79: 275–277.

Sumner, E.L. 1936. Special report on a wildlife study of the High Sierra in Sequoia and Yosemite National Parks and adjacent territory. Washington, DC: National Park Service.

Sutton, S. 2004. Outdoor recreation planning frameworks: an overview of best practices and comparison with Department of Conservation (New Zealand) planning processes. In: Smith, K.A.; Schott, C., eds. Proceedings of the New Zealand tourism and hospitality research conference. Wellington, New Zealand: University of Victoria: 407–423.

Troy, L.R. 1998. Recent human migration to the interior Columbia basin and implications for natural resource management. Missoula, MT: School of Forestry, University of Montana. 71 p.

U.S. Department of Agriculture, Forest Service [USDA FS]. 1982. ROS users guide. Washington, DC. 37 p.

U.S. Department of Agriculture, Forest Service [USDA FS]. 1990. ROS primer and field guide. R6-REC-021-90. Portland, OR: Pacific Northwest Regional Office.

U.S. Department of Agriculture, Forest Service [USDA FS]. 2001. The built environment image guide for the national forests and grasslands. FS-710. Washington, DC.

U.S. Department of Commerce, Bureau of the Census [USDC Bureau of the Census]. 2002. Population profile of the United States. www.census.gov/population/www/pop-profice/profile2000.html#cont. (April 2, 2006).

U.S. Department of Commerce, Bureau of Economic Analysis [BEA]. 2006. Regional economic analysis. www.bea.gov/bea/regional/bearfacts/action.cfm?fips=57017&areatype=57017&yearin=2003. (April 2, 2006).

U.S. Department of the Interior, Bureau of Land Management [USDI BLM]. 1998. Grand Staircase Escalante National Monument draft management plan draft environmental impact statement. www.ut.blm.gov/monument/planning-draft-eis.php. (July 17, 2006).

U.S. Department of the Interior, National Park Service [USDI NPS]. 1997. VERP: A summary of the Visitor Experience and Resource Protection (VERP) framework. Denver, CO. 103 p.

Wagar, J.A. 1963. Campgrounds for many tastes. Res. Pap. INT-6. Ogden, UT: U.S. Department of Agriculture, Forest Service, Intermountain Forest and Range Experiment Station. 10 p.

Wagar, J.A. 1964. The carrying capacity of wildlands for recreation. Forest Science Monograph 7. Washington, DC: Society of American Foresters: 1-23.

Wagar, J.A. 1966. Quality in outdoor recreation. Trends in Parks and Recreation. 3(3): 9–12.

Wagar, J.A. 1974. Recreational carrying capacity reconsidered. Journal of Forestry. 72(5): 274–278.

Washburne, R.F. 1981. Carrying capacity assessment and recreational use in the national wilderness preservation system. Journal of Soil and Water Conservation. 36(3): 162–166.

Washburne, R.F. 1982. Wilderness recreation carrying capacity: Are numbers necessary? Journal of Forestry. 80: 726–728.

Wearing, S.; Archer, D. 2003. An interpretation opportunity spectrum: a new approach to the planning and provision of interpretation in protected areas. In: Braithwaite, R.W.; Braithwaite, R.L., eds. Riding the wave of tourism and hospitality research. Proceedings of the Council of Australian, University tourism and hospitality education conference. Lismore, Australia: Southern Cross University: 1–18

Weick, K.E.; Sutcliffe, K.M. 2001. Managing the unexpected: assuring high performance in an age of complexity. San Francisco: Jossey-Bass. 200 p.

Whitmore, J.; Borrie, W.T.; Watson, A. 2005. Bob Marshall Wilderness Complex 2004 visitor study. Missoula, MT: College of Forestry and Conservation, The University of Montana. 148 p.

Wilderness Act of 1964; 16 U.S.C. 1121 (note), 1131–1136.

Wondolleck, J.M. 1988. Public lands conflict and resolution: managing National Forest disputes. New York: Plenum Press. 284 p.

Wondolleck, J.M.; Yaffee, S.L. 2000. Making collaboration work: lessons from innovation in natural resource management. Washington, DC: Island Press. 227 p.

www.ingramcontent.com/pod-product-compliance
Lightning Source LLC
Chambersburg PA
CBHW080258290526
45790CB00005B/1851